SCIENCE JOU

McGRAW-HILL

SCIENCE

GRADE 4

Mc Graw Hill **McGraw-Hill School Division**

New York   Farmington

Table of Contents

Investigate Why Things Sink or Float

Why do some things float and some things sink? How can some things float lower than others?

Write a possible explanation:

_____

Think of a sentence about sinking and floating that you can test, like: Heavier things sink, and lighter things float.

Materials

- plastic film canister
- ball of modeling clay
- empty plastic soda bottle (with top)
- large metal lid for mayonnaise, jam, or pickle jar
- tub or bucket of water
- balance
- sand or salt
- ruler

Procedures

1. Fill the sink or tub with water.

2. Put the tops tightly on the empty canister and soda bottle.

3. **Predict** Weigh the canister, soda bottle, lid, and ball of modeling clay, and measure the lengths and widths. Discuss which ones you think will sink and which will float? Why? Write your ideas.

   _____

   _____

4. **Observe** Place the objects in the water one by one. Record whether they sink or float.

   _____

5. **Experiment** Now try to change the results any way you can. Make just one change at a time. Test the canister and bottle when they are filled with water, sand, or salt. Change the shape of the modeling clay. Each time you make a change, weigh and measure the items. Record the results.

   _____

   _____

Conclude and Apply

1. **Draw Conclusions** Did the heavier items always sink? Why?

_____

_____

2. **Draw Conclusions** Did the height and width of the objects make a difference? If so, how?

_____

_____

3. Could you make the modeling clay float by changing its shape?

_____

_____

❓ Inquiry

Think of your own questions that you might like to test using the objects and the tub or bucket of water.

My Question Is:

_____

_____

How I Can Test It:

_____

_____

My Results Are:

_____

_____

Investigate What Living Things Are Made Of

Hypothesize Sometimes it is hard to tell if an object is living or nonliving. However, living things have certain parts in common. What might they be?

Write a **Hypothesis:**

_____

_____

Observe parts of an onion plant with a microscope and a hand lens.

Materials

- onion plant
- hand lens
- prepared slides of onion skin and leaf
- microscope

Procedures

1. **Observe** On a separate sheet of paper, draw the whole onion plant. Label its parts. Write down how each part might help the plant live.

2. **Observe** Ask your teacher to cut the plant lengthwise. On another sheet of paper, draw and label what you see.

3. **Observe** Observe a small section of onion skin and a thin piece of a leaf with the hand lens. On another sheet of paper, draw what you see.

4. **Observe** Use the microscope to look at the onion skin and the leaf section. Use high and low power. On another sheet of paper, draw what you see.

Conclude and Apply

1. **Communicate** What did you see when you examined the onion skin and leaf with the hand lens and the microscope. Make a table or chart.

2. **Compare and Contrast** How are your observations of the onion skin and leaf alike and different?

_____

_____

_____

_____

3. **Draw Conclusions** What do the parts of the onion plant seem to be made of?

_____

Going Further: Problem Solving

4. **Experiment** Do you think you would see similar structures if you observed a part of the root? How could you find out?

_____

_____

❓ Inquiry

Think of your own questions about parts of plants that you might like to test. Would other plants have structures similar to the ones you saw in the onion plant?

My Question Is:

_____

_____

How I Can Test It:

_____

_____

My Results Are:

_____

_____

Putting It All Together

Hypothesize What body parts work together to allow you to perform a simple task like writing?

Write a **Hypothesis:**

_____

_____

Materials

• pen or pencil

Procedures

1. Write your name. _____

2. **Infer** As you write, think about what each body part, organ, and organ system is doing.

_____

Conclude and Apply

1. **Communicate** Write a paragraph that tells what organs you were using. Consider the organs you use to see, touch, breathe, and think.

_____

_____

_____

_____

2. **Draw Conclusions** How did your body parts and organs work together to allow you to write?

_____

_____

_____

_____

_____

Going Further Think of another task, and identify the body parts involved in performing that task. Write down the task and the body parts used.

My Hypothesis Is:

_____

_____

My Experiment Is:

_____

My Results Are:

_____

_____

Investigate How Plant and Animal Cells Are Different

Hypothesize How could you find out how plant and animal cells are different?

Write a **Hypothesis:**

_____

_____

Use a microscope to look at plant and animal cells to find out if they are different. The plant cells are from a freshwater plant called *Elodea* (i lō´dē ə). The animal cells are cheek cells that line the inside of a person's mouth.

Materials

• prepared slides of an *Elodea* leaf and human cheek cells   • microscope

Procedures

1. Place the slide of *Elodea* on the microscope stage.

2. Observe Focus through the top layers of cells using low power. Focus on one plant cell. On a separate piece of paper, draw the plant cell.

3. Observe Place the prepared slide of cheek cells on the microscope stage. Focus on one cheek cell using low power. Draw the cheek cell on a separate piece of paper.

4. Communicate Observe the cells and fill in the table below.

CHARACTERISTICS OF PLANT AND ANIMAL CELLS			
	Shape	**Color**	**Cell Structures Present**
Plant cell			
Animal cell			

Conclude and Apply

1. Observe What did you see when you observed the *Elodea* cells?

_____

2. Observe What did you see when you observed the cheek cells?

_____

3. Compare and Contrast How are the *Elodea* and cheek cells similar and different?

_____

_____

4. Compare and Contrast How does the *Elodea* cell compare with the onion skin cell you observed in Topic 1?

_____

_____

Going Further: Apply

5. Infer How do you think scientists use cell structure in classifying organisms?

_____

Inquiry

Think of your own question about cells that you can investigate. How do different kinds of plant and animal cells compare?

My Question Is:

_____

How I Can Test It:

_____

My Results Are:

_____

_____

Making a Model

Modeling Plant and Animal Cells

Most cells are too small for you to see without a microscope, but you can build models of cells. Models are three-dimensional copies or drawings of real things. A model can help you see how something looks or behaves.

Materials

- small plastic bags with twist ties
- beads or marbles
- lima beans
- tape
- scissors

- prepared, light-colored gelatin
- green jelly beans or olives
- marshmallows
- clear plastic box

Procedures

▨ **Safety** Do not eat any of the activity materials!

1. **Plan** Make a list of parts of an animal cell. Name a material to stand for each part.

   _____

   _____

   _____

2. **Make a Model** Build an animal cell using the materials you named for each part.

3. **Repeat** Follow the same process for a plant-cell model. How will it be different from your animal-cell model?

   _____

   _____

4. **Communicate** Compare your cell models. Record your observations.

   _____

   _____

Conclude and Apply

1. **Explain** How did building a model help you understand the shape of each type of cell?

   _____

   _____

2. **Observe** What cell structures do your models have?

   _____

   _____

   _____

3. **Compare and Contrast** What structures do both your models share? What structures don't they share?

   _____

   _____

   _____

4. **Infer** In what ways do you think your cell models are similar to real cells? In what ways are they different?

   _____

   _____

Design Your Own Experiment

How Are Organisms Classified?

Hypothesize What characteristics do you think scientists use to classify living things?

Write a **Hypothesis:**

_____

_____

Materials

• reference books

Procedures

1. **Observe** Choose eight very different organisms that you would like to classify and learn more about. You may choose the ones you see on the third page of this Explore Activity. Record their names.

_____

_____

2. **Collect Data** What would you like to know about your organisms? Where would you look to find the information? Design a table to record the information.

3. **Classify** Try to place all of the organisms into groups. What characteristics did you use to help you make your choices?

_____

_____

Conclude and Apply

1. Identify How many groups were formed? What were the major characteristics of the organisms in each group?

_____

_____

2. Explain What organisms were placed in each group?

_____

_____

3. Communicate Make a list of the characteristics of the organisms in each group.

_____

_____

Going Further: Apply

4. Repeat Test your classification system by adding a new organism. Does it fit in a group? Why or why not? If not, what changes could you make to your system so that it would fit?

_____

_____

Inquiry

Think of your own questions concerning classification that you would like to research.

My Question Is:

_____

How I Can Test It:

_____

My Results Are:

_____

_____

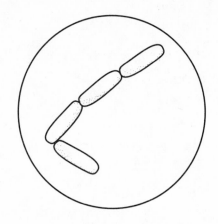

_____

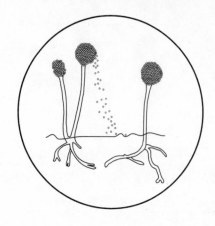

_____

_____

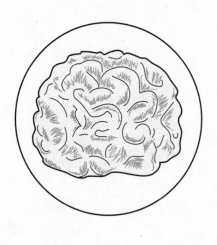

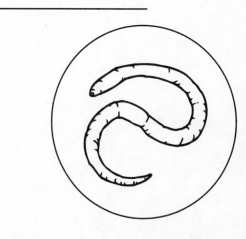

_____

_____

_____

Classifying

Classifying Leaves

When you organize toys or living things into groups, you are classifying. When you classify, you organize things into smaller groups based on their traits. This skill is important not only in science. People classify things every day. Classifying helps make things easier to study and understand. To practice this skill, you will classify leaves according to different traits.

Materials

• 10 leaves or leaf pictures shown on the third page of this Skill Builder

• ruler

Procedures

1. **Observe** Spread out the leaves (or leaf pictures). Observe the traits they share, such as size, color, shape, and so on. Record the traits.

_____

2. **Classify** Choose one trait, such as color, that you recorded. Organize all ten leaves based on that trait. Draw the way your leaves are organized. You may use a table.

3. Repeat Follow the same procedure for two other traits you recorded.

Conclude and Apply

1. Identify In how many different ways were you able to classify
the leaves?

_____

2. Compare and Contrast How did your classification system differ from
other students' systems? In what ways were they similar?

_____

_____

3. Classify Give some examples of how other things are classified. Use
a kitchen, bedroom, closet, or supermarket.

_____

_____

4. Draw Conclusions How do you think using a worldwide classification
system might help scientists identify and understand organisms?

_____

_____

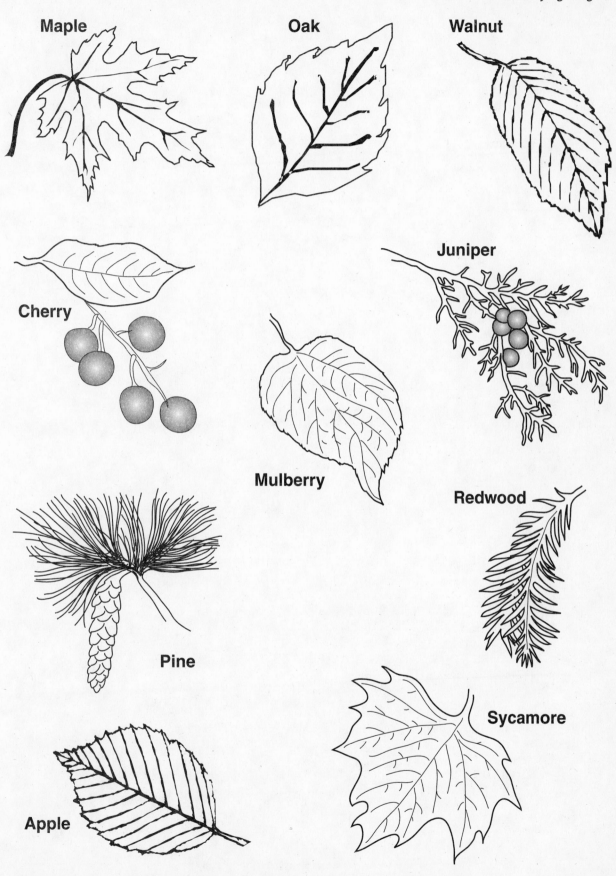

Maple

Oak

Walnut

Cherry

Mulberry

Juniper

Pine

Redwood

Apple

Sycamore

Investigate Using Skeletons to Compare Organisms

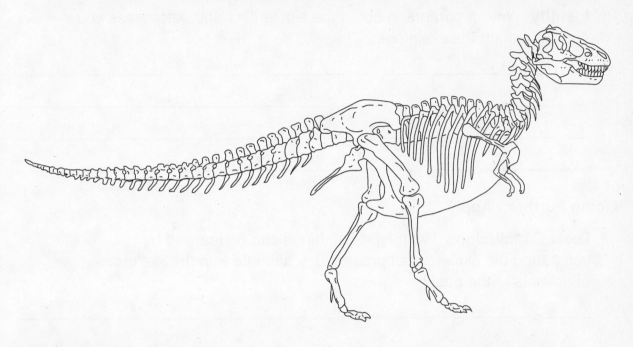

Hypothesize Does this dinosaur skeleton remind you of any animals alive today? What might be learned from comparing the bones of past and present-day animals?

Write a **Hypothesis:**

_____

_____

Carefully observe and compare the three skeletons.

Materials

• ruler, pencil, and paper, or computer with charting program

Procedures

1. **Compare and Contrast** Compare the picture of the dinosaur skeleton with the bird and reptile skeletons on the third page of this Explore Activity.

2. **Communicate** On a separate piece of paper, make a chart that lists the similarities and differences. Use a computer if you like.

Conclude and Apply

1. Identify Write a paragraph about the similarities and differences you noticed among the skeletons.

_____

_____

_____

_____

Going Further: Apply

2. Draw Conclusions What types of things can be learned by comparing the skeletons of present-day animals with the skeletons of animals of the past?

_____

_____

? Inquiry

Think of your own questions about how animals have changed that you might research. Would you like to compare an ancient and present-day animal?

My Question Is:

_____

How I Can Test It:

_____

My Results Are:

_____

_____

This is a skeleton of a bird.

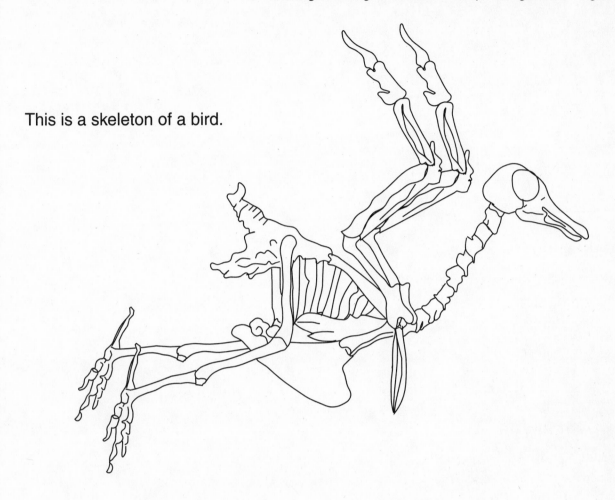

This is a skeleton of a reptile.

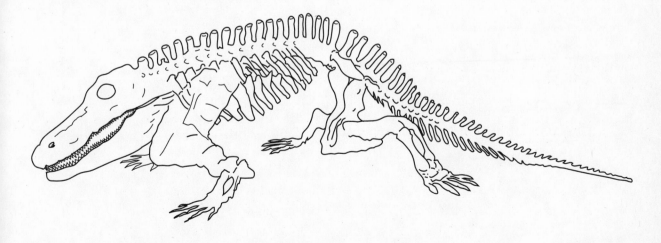

Older and Younger

Hypothesize Relative dating is placing things in order from oldest to youngest. What do you look for to help you decide which is older and younger?

Write a **Hypothesis:**

_____

_____

Materials

• 4 books   • 2 pieces of paper   • scissors   • pen or pencil

Procedures

1. **Observe** Cut a piece of paper into four pieces. Draw a "fossil" on each piece. Place one fossil inside the front cover of each book. Stack the books.

2. **Interpret Data** Challenge your partner to find the fossils and arrange them in order of which is "oldest" and "youngest." Record any observations you make.

_____

_____

3. **Repeat** Switch roles and repeat the activity.

Conclude and Apply

1. **Explain** What did the books represent?

_____

2. **Identify** Which fossil was oldest? Youngest? What evidence helped you decide?

_____

_____

_____

Going Further Carbon dating is a technique used to approximate how long ago an organism died. Research and explain carbon dating.

My Hypothesis Is:

_____

_____

My Experiment Is:

_____

_____

_____

My Results Are:

_____

_____

_____

_____

Investigate How Living and Nonliving Things Interact

Hypothesize The key to an organism's survival is how it interacts with other living and nonliving things. What might these interactions be?

Write a **Hypothesis:**

_____

_____

_____

Build a terrarium as a model of an environment. Observe it to see how living things interact with each other and their surroundings.

Materials

- prepared terrarium container
- plastic spoon
- ruler
- water mister
- small plants and animals
- grass seeds, rocks, twigs, sticks, bark, dried grass

Procedures

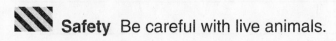 **Safety** Be careful with live animals.

1. **Make a Model** Landscape your terrarium. Put taller plants in the back. Spread grass seed and any rocks, twigs, or other things you like.

2. If you add small animals, such as earthworms, sow bugs, or snails, add a water dish.

3. **Measure** Make a data table on a separate piece of paper. Record the height of each plant. Measure the plants in two weeks, and record the data. Make a bar graph.

4. Place the terrarium in a lighted area. Avoid direct sunlight.

5. **Communicate** On a new page, draw a diagram of your terrarium. Draw arrows to show how the organisms depend on each other.

Conclude and Apply

1. Classify What are the living and nonliving things in the terrarium?

_____

2. Infer Why should the terrarium not be placed in direct sunlight?

_____

_____

Going Further: Apply

3. Observe Continue to maintain and observe your terrarium. Did anything unusual happen? Why do you think this happened?

_____

_____

Inquiry

Think of how you might change the terrarium ecosystem. Would you like to add or remove a living or nonliving thing?

My Question Is:

_____

_____

How I Can Test It:

_____

My Results Are:

_____

A Misty Experiment

Hypothesize What kinds of habitats do different organisms prefer? Form a hypothesis. Use your terrarium to find out.

Write a **Hypothesis:**

_____

_____

Materials

• Explore Activity terrarium   • water mister   • water

Procedures

1. Lightly spray one side of your terrarium each day for one week. Leave the other side dry.

2. **Observe** Record your observations of how the individual organisms react each day.

Day	Observations
1	
2	
3	
4	
5	

Conclude and Apply

1. **Predict** Which organisms preferred the wet side of the terrarium? Where would you expect these organisms to live in the wild? Explain.

_____

_____

2. Predict Which organisms preferred the dry side of the terrarium? Where would you expect these organisms to live in the wild? Explain.

_____

_____

Going Further The Misty Experiment used examples of wet and dry climates. Can you create a representation of a warmer or cooler climate or growing conditions containing more or less light? Describe and perform an experiment to test a specified growing environment.

My Hypothesis Is:

_____

_____

My Experiment Is:

_____

_____

_____

_____

_____

_____

My Results Are:

_____

_____

Observe a Decomposer

Hypothesize What do you think molds need to grow?

Write a **Hypothesis:**

_____

Materials

- 5 sealable plastic bags
- 4 food samples
- piece of cardboard
- warm water
- hand lens
- marking pen

Procedures

Safety Do not open the bags after you seal them.

1. Moisten the food samples. Place each in a labeled plastic bag. Put a piece of cardboard in a bag.

2. Seal the bags, and place them in a warm, dark place.

3. **Observe** Record your daily observations.

OBSERVATIONS					
Day	Card-board				
1					
2					
3					
4					
5					

Conclude and Apply

1. **Observe** On which samples did mold grow?

_____

2. **Infer** Will molds grow on any type of material? Explain how the cardboard helped you answer this question.

_____

_____

3. **Observe** How did the molds change the foods?

_____

_____

Going Further Several methods are used to deter the growth of molds on food and extend the time that foods are safe for consumption. Refrigerating, or cooling food slows the growth of molds. Pickling and salting foods create an environment that molds cannot survive. Test these methods of food preservation.

My Hypothesis Is:

_____

_____

My Experiment Is:

_____

_____

_____

_____

_____

My Results Are:

_____

_____

Investigate How You Can Describe It

Hypothesize How could you investigate a "mystery substance" to determine if it belongs in the museum?

Write a **Hypothesis:**

_____

_____

Observe, test and describe a "mystery substance" in as much detail as you can.

Materials

• mystery substance
• assorted tools

• small bowl
• water

Procedures

Safety Do not taste the mystery substance.

Observe Record as many observations of the mystery substance as you can. Here are some ideas.

• How does it look, feel, and smell? Will anything stick to it? Can you use it like glue? Does it work like a magnet?

• Use tools to test it. Is it strong, brittle, or flexible? Can you mold it? Does it shatter or bend?

• What happens if you put some in water?

• Will it copy pictures from the comics?

_____

_____

_____

_____

_____

Conclude and Apply

1. Communicate List five words or phrases that you would use to describe the mystery substance.

_____

_____

2. Explain Do you think the mystery substance belongs in the Museum That Matters? Why or why not?

_____

_____

Going Further: Apply

3. Compare List five words or phrases that you would use to describe your shoe. How are the words like those you used to describe the substance?

_____

_____

❓ Inquiry

Think of your own questions about the mystery substance that you might like to test. What other ways can you test the mystery substance?

My Question Is:

_____

_____

How I Can Test It:

_____

_____

My Results Are:

_____

Identifying Matter

Hypothesize Is air matter? Use what you know about matter to design an experiment to find out.

Write a **Hypothesis:**

_____

_____

Materials

• 2 balloons   • meterstick   • string   • scissors

Procedures

Safety Use the scissors carefully!

1. **Experiment** Using the materials, design an experiment to determine whether air has mass. Record your setup.

_____

_____

_____

_____

_____

2. **Use Variables** Test the experiment. Record each step, all of your observations, and your results.

_____

_____

Conclude and Apply

1. **Draw Conclusions** Is air matter? What evidence do you have to support your conclusion?

_____

_____

_____

2. Infer Dan blew up a balloon until it burst. Does the broken
balloon support the idea that air is matter or the idea that air is
non-matter? Explain.

_____

_____

_____

Going Further What other evidence do you have that air is matter?
Think about the effects of moving air, such as wind. What happens to the
objects when the fan is turned on?

My Hypothesis Is:

_____

My Experiment Is:

_____

_____

My Results Are:

_____

_____

Design Your Own Experiment

How Can You Measure Matter?

Hypothesize What if you are buying or selling items in a marketplace where everyone measures things in his or her own way? How could you solve the problems this causes?

Write a **Hypothesis:**

_____

Materials

- variety of objects that can be "sold"   • play money

Procedures

1. **Plan** Decide who will be the merchant and who will be the customer. The merchant will set up goods and determine their prices. The customer will decide on the types and quantities of things you want to buy.

2. **Communicate** Pretend to buy and sell things. Compare your ideas of what each quantity should be. Who is at an advantage and who is at a disadvantage each time? Record your "measurements" and observations.

_____

_____

3. **Use Numbers** Calculate the price for each purchase. Record the calculations and prices.

_____

_____

4. **Communicate** Work together to agree on how to measure items.

Conclude and Apply

1. **Communicate** In the first part of the activity, you did not have a system of set measurements. How did you know if you were selling your things too cheaply? How did you know if you were paying a fair price or not?

_____

_____

2. **Explain** Do you think it is important to agree on how to measure things? Why or why not?

_____

_____

_____

Going Further: Problem Solving

3. **Infer** How would having set measurements help you as a merchant? How would it *not* help you?

_____

_____

? Inquiry

Think of your own questions that you might like to test. What other standard measures could you try to do without?

My Question Is:

_____

How I Can Test It:

_____

My Results Are:

_____

_____

Inferring

Examine If Shape Affects Volume

Does the volume of an object change if its shape changes? In this activity you will use water to help you find the volume of clay molded into different shapes. You will use your observations and measurements to infer the answer to the question. When you infer, you use observations to figure something out.

Materials

- clay
- water
- paper towels

- graduated cylinder
- string

Procedures

1. Fill the graduated cylinder with 50 mL of water.

2. Make a solid figure out of the clay. Press the string into it.

3. **Observe** Hold the string. Lower the clay into the water until it is completely covered. Carefully observe and record the new water level.

   _____

   _____

4. Remove the figure. Rearrange it to make a different shape. Do not add or take away any clay.

5. Repeat step 3 and record your measurements.

   _____

   _____

Conclude and Apply

1. **Use Numbers** What was the volume of each figure? How did you find out?

   _____

   _____

   _____

2. Infer Does an object's volume change when you change its shape? How do you know?

_____

_____

_____

3. Repeat Repeat the procedure with a third shape of clay to verify your results.

_____

_____

4. Infer Toy A raised the water level in a tank 1 cm. Toy B raised the water level 2 cm. What can you infer about their volumes?

_____

_____

_____

Comparing Densities

Hypothesize How can you compare densities of different items?

Write a **Hypothesis:**

_____

_____

Materials

• equal-sized samples of a wooden block, clay, and foam
• pan balance
• metric ruler

Procedures

1. **Observe** Does each sample have the same volume? How can you tell?

_____

_____

2. **Predict** Which sample do you think has the greatest density? The least?

_____

_____

3. **Compare** Use the balance to compare the masses of the samples. Record the data in the table below.

Material	Mass
wood	
clay	
foam	

Conclude and Apply

1. Compare Rank the items from greatest to least density.

_____

_____

2. Infer Why would you need information about both mass and volume
to compare density?

_____

_____

Going Further Does the density of a material change when it is made into
a different shape? Write down your thoughts. How can you verify your
ideas using the clay sample?

My Hypothesis Is:

_____

_____

My Experiment Is:

_____

_____

_____

My Results Are:

_____

_____

_____

Investigate How You Can Classify Matter

Hypothesize How would you design a classification system for ten items? How can you test your ideas?

Write a **Hypothesis:**

_____

_____

Design and test a classification system for a group of ten items.

Materials

- 10 assorted items
- index cards

Procedures

1. **Communicate** Write the name of each item on an index card.

2. **Classify** Sort the items into groups based on properties you can observe. Record the properties. Try to use a system like the one below.

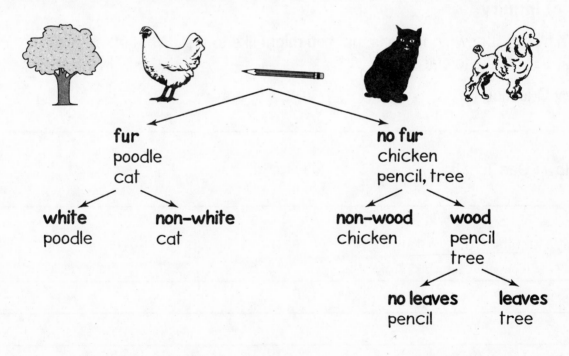

_____

_____

Conclude and Apply

1. Communicate What properties did you use to classify the items?

_____

_____

2. Communicate Were you able to place all the items into the groups? Why or why not?

_____

_____

Going Further: Problem Solving

3. Classify Can you classify each object in its own group? Why or why not? Would changing your system allow you to do so? How?

_____

_____

Inquiry

Think of your own questions that you might like to test. What other things would you like to classify?

My Question Is:

_____

How I Can Test It:

_____

My Results Are:

_____

_____

_____

Mix and Unmix

Hypothesize How can you use physical properties to separate the parts of a mixture?

Write a **Hypothesis:**

_____

_____

Materials

- goggles
- mixture from your teacher
- piece of dark paper
- plastic funnel
- tweezers or forceps
- container
- magnet
- filter paper
- water

Procedures

Safety Wear goggles.

Observe Design an experiment to separate the mixture. Hint: You may need to use more than one method or to repeat some methods more than once. Record your observations and results.

_____

_____

_____

_____

_____

Conclude and Apply

1. **Observe** Were you able to completely separate the mixture? How do you know?

_____

_____

_____

2. Hypothesize How could you separate a mixture of white sand and salt? Test your ideas.

_____

_____

_____

Going Further Sometimes it is not obvious that something is a mixture. Heavy cream contains butterfat and water. Can you separate the water from the butterfat in heavy cream? Write down your idea and try it. The separation need not be complete.

My Hypothesis Is:

_____

_____

My Experiment Is:

_____

_____

_____

My Results Are:

_____

_____

Investigate What Causes the Change

Hypothesize Compare the Statue of Liberty with clean copper. What do you think caused the statue to turn green?

Write a **Hypothesis:**

_____

_____

Investigate the conditions that cause a penny to change.

Materials

- goggles
- 1 tsp. vinegar
- modeling clay

- shiny penny
- petri dish or 10-oz clear plastic glass
- 10-oz clear plastic glass or plastic wrap

Procedures

 Safety Wear goggles.

1. Put a small wad of modeling clay on the bottom of the petri dish or plastic glass.

2. Wedge the penny in the clay so that it is vertical.

3. Add 1 tsp. of vinegar to the petri dish or glass. Cover the petri dish with the plastic glass. If you put the penny in the glass, cover the glass tightly with plastic wrap.

4. **Predict** What do you think will happen to the penny?
   Record your prediction.

_____

_____

Conclude and Apply

1. **Observe** What happens to the penny after one hour?
   After three hours? Overnight? Record your observations.

_____

_____

2. Compare How is this penny different from the penny that your teacher soaked in vinegar overnight?

_____

3. Hypothesize What do you think caused the changes to your penny but not the soaked penny?

_____

_____

_____

Going Further: Problem Solving

4. Experiment Do you think other materials would change also? Repeat the activity using a paper clip.

_____

Inquiry

Think of your own questions that you might like to test. What other substances might cause similar reactions?

My Question Is:

_____

How I Can Test It:

_____

_____

My Results Are:

_____

_____

Preventing Chemical Change

Hypothesize Why do you think most pennies you use every day aren't green?

Write a **Hypothesis:**

_____

_____

_____

Materials

- goggles
- modeling clay
- 1 tsp. vinegar
- other materials as needed

- petri dish or 10-oz clear-plastic glass
- 3 shiny pennies
- 10-oz clear-plastic glass or plastic wrap

Procedures

Safety Wear goggles.

1. **Hypothesize** Set up the materials as in the Explore Activity. Think about a different thing you can do to each penny to keep it from turning green. Record your ideas.

_____

_____

2. **Experiment** Test your ideas. Record your results.

_____

_____

_____

Conclude and Apply

1. **Compare** Make a class table of the results for each test. What kept the pennies from turning green?

_____

_____

2. Infer What do you think prevents the pennies you use every day from turning green?

_____

_____

Going Further Is there more than one reason why the pennies we use every day are not green? Is the environment where you live very damaging to pennies? Is the coating that forms on everyday pennies protective?

My Hypothesis Is:

_____

_____

My Experiment Is:

_____

_____

_____

_____

_____

_____

My Results Are:

_____

_____

_____

Experimenting

How Heat Energy Affects Evaporation

Sometimes the only way to answer a question is to perform an experiment. In an experiment you first form a hypothesis. Then you set up conditions to test your hypothesis. Follow the steps below to test how heat energy affects evaporation.

Materials

- 3 paper-towel pieces
- three 10-oz clear-plastic glasses
- clock or watch
- container of water

- 3 rubber bands
- thermometer
- desk lamp

Procedures

1. Place a wet paper towel across the top of each plastic glass. Secure each with a rubber band.

2. **Predict** Place one glass where you think the paper towel will dry fastest. Place another where you think it will dry slower. Place the third where you think it will dry slowest.

3. **Measure** Use the thermometer to measure the temperature near each glass. Record the temperatures.

_____

_____

_____

4. Record the time you start timing. Then touch each paper towel every two minutes. Record the time the first paper towel is dry.

_____

_____

_____

5. **Repeat** Repeat Step 4 until another towel is dry.

Conclude and Apply

1. Interpret In which place did a paper towel dry the fastest? What was the temperature?

_____

_____

2. Interpret In which place did a paper towel dry the slowest? What was the temperature?

_____

_____

3. Infer Would water evaporate from a paper towel as fast if you put another inverted glass on top of it? Try it.

_____

_____

_____

_____

_____

Investigate How Fat Keeps Mammals Warm

Hypothesize Whales have a thick layer of body fat beneath their skin. Do you think it keeps them warm in the freezing waters?

Write a **Hypothesis:**

_____

_____

Test if a layer of fat can help keep your hand warm in cold water.

Materials

- plastic bag containing lard or solid vegetable shortening
- 2 vinyl surgical gloves
- bucket or pan of ice water
- timer or watch with second hand
- paper towels

Procedures

1. **Collect Data** Put on one glove. Ask your partner to time how long you can comfortably keep your hand in the ice water. Record the results.

   _____

2. Move your gloved hand around in the bag of lard to coat it well. Be sure to spread the lard over your entire hand and between your fingers.

3. **Collect Data** Ask your partner to time how long you can comfortably keep your lard-coated hand in the ice water. Record the results.

   _____

4. **Collect Data** Trade places and let your partner repeat the procedure.

   _____

5. **Use Numbers** Take an average of both of your results.

   _____

Conclude and Apply

1. Communicate How long on average were you able to keep your hand in the ice water in step 1? In step 3?

_____

2. Infer What role do you think the lard played in keeping your hand warm?

_____

Going Further: Problem Solving

3. Infer If the lard represents a whale's blubber, how might it help the whale survive?

_____

_____

Inquiry

Think of your own questions that you might like to test. What other forms of insulation would you like to test?

My Question Is:

_____

_____

How I Can Test It:

_____

_____

My Results Are:

_____

_____

Bag in a Bag

Hypothesize What happens when objects of different temperatures touch?

Write a **Hypothesis:**

_____

_____

Materials

- small sealable plastic bag containing 1 c of ice water
- large sealable plastic bag containing 1 c of very warm water
- paper towels
- thermometer
- watch or timer

Procedures

Safety Be careful when handling the bags of water.

1. **Collect Data** Record the temperatures of the ice water and the very warm water.

_____

2. **Predict** Seal the small bag. Place it in the large bag, then seal it. Predict how the water temperatures will change with time.

_____

_____

3. **Collect Data** Wait two minutes, then take the temperature of the water in each bag. Repeat this several times. Record the data.

_____

_____

Conclude and Apply

1. **Observe** What was the final temperature of the water in each bag?

_____

_____

2. Infer How can you explain your findings?

_____

_____

_____

Going Further Can you feel differences in the rates of heat transfer between different materials? Write and conduct an experiment.

My Hypothesis Is:

_____

_____

My Experiment Is:

_____

_____

_____

_____

_____

My Results Are:

_____

_____

_____

Matter and Heat

Hypothesize What happens to air when it is heated?

Write a **Hypothesis:**

_____

_____

_____

Materials

- goggles
- blow dryer
- ruler
- timer or watch with second hand
- inflated balloon
- string
- marking pen

Procedures

Safety Wear goggles.

1. **Measure** Use the string and ruler to measure the balloon.
   Mark the spot where you measured it. Record the data.

   _____

2. **Measure** Heat the balloon with the blow dryer for one minute.
   Measure the distance around the balloon at the marked spot. Record
   the data.

   _____

Conclude and Apply

1. How did heat affect the size of the balloon?

   _____

2. **Explain** What happens to the air particles in the balloon when it
   is heated?

   _____

   _____

Going Further Can you demonstrate a change in volume with
temperature using the balloon and a different type of heat transfer?
Write and conduct an experiment.

My Hypothesis Is:

_____

_____

My Experiment Is:

_____

_____

_____

_____

My Results Are:

_____

_____

_____

Investigate What It Takes to Move Something

Hypothesize How could the movers get a chest to the third floor?

Write a **Hypothesis:**

_____

Use a pulley to lift a book.

Materials
- pulley
- 2 pieces of rope (thick string)
- book
- spring scale

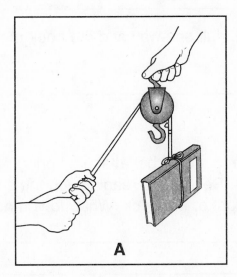

A

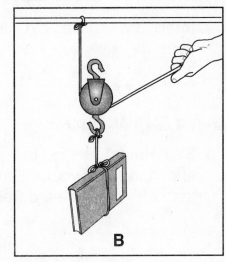

B

Procedures

1. Tie the longer piece of cord around the book. Have a partner hold the pulley as shown in figure A. Thread the cord through the pulley's groove.

2. **Observe** Pull down on the cord. What happens? Draw the pulley, cord, and book system. Use arrows to show the direction you pull and the direction the book moves.

3. **Observe** Attach one end of the second cord passing through the pulley to something that won't move, as shown in figure B. Attach the book to the hook on the pulley. Pull up on the other end of the cord. What happens to the pulley? What happens to the book? Draw the system. Use arrows to show the direction you pull and the direction the book and pulley move.

Conclude and Apply

1. **Compare and Contrast** Was it easier to lift the book in step 2 or 3? Why do you think so?

   _____

   _____

2. **Infer** In which step did you pull one way and the book moved the opposite way?

   _____

Going Further: Apply

3. **Experiment** Repeat the procedures but attach a spring scale to the end of the cord you pull on. Record the readings on the scale for each trial. Also measure the weight of the book. What do you notice?

   _____

   _____

   _____

Inquiry

What other loads would you like to test with the pulley systems?
Write and conduct an experiment.

My Question Is:

_____

_____

How I Can Test It:

_____

_____

My Results Are:

_____

_____

Make Levers

Hypothesize What happens to the direction of the force when you use a lever?

Write a **Hypothesis:**

_____

_____

Materials

- book
- ruler
- pencil

Procedures

1. **Make a Model** Place about an inch of the ruler under the edge of the book. Place the pencil under the ruler close to the book.

2. Push down on the other end of the ruler. Record what happens.

_____

3. Place as much of the ruler under the book as fits. Remove the pencil.

4. Lift up on the end of the ruler sticking out from under the book. Record what happens.

_____

Conclude and Apply

1. When you pushed down in step 2, which way did the lever push?

_____

2. **Draw Conclusions** Can a lever change the direction of the force? Explain.

_____

3. What kind of lever did you make? Explain.

_____

Going Further Demonstrate the mechanical advantage of a second-class
lever. Where is the load located when the effort force is the smallest?
Where is the load located when the effort force is the greatest?
Write and conduct an experiment.

My Hypothesis Is:

_____

_____

My Experiment Is:

_____

_____

_____

_____

_____

_____

_____

_____

_____

_____

_____

My Results Are:

_____

_____

Investigate How You Interpret Clues in Rocks

Hypothesize What evidence can you find in a rock that tells about its formation?

Write a **Hypothesis:**

_____

_____

Infer how these rocks were formed by observing their physical properties.

Materials

• 5 different rock samples   • hand lens

Procedures

1. **Observe** Carefully observe each rock. Describe and record its properties. Look for properties such as color, hardness, texture, and shininess. Is it made of smaller particles that you can see? Does it have any layers?

_____

_____

2. **Observe** Use a hand lens to observe each rock sample. Record your observations.

_____

_____

3. **Communicate** Compare your observations with those of your classmates. Make a class list of all the properties you observed.

Conclude and Apply

1. **Infer** Which rocks may have formed from sand or gravel? What evidence supports your answer?

_____

_____

2. Infer Which rock may have formed on an ocean bottom? What evidence supports your answer?

_____

_____

3. Compare samples B and E. How are they alike? How are they different?

_____

_____

_____

Going Further: Problem Solving

4. Infer How do you think sample E formed? Why do you think so?

_____

_____

_____

❓ Inquiry

Think of your own questions you might like to test. What other properties can tell about a rock's formation?

My Question Is:

_____

How I Can Test It:

_____

_____

My Results Are:

_____

Identifying Minerals

Hypothesize How can you tell minerals apart?

Write a **Hypothesis:**

_____

_____

Materials

- 5 mineral samples, labeled 1 to 5
- hardness testers—copper penny, your fingernail
- goggles (for "Going Further")
- streak plate

Procedures

Analyze Use the tools and the table on the next page to identify each mineral sample. Write the properties and names on a separate piece of paper.

Conclude and Apply

Evaluate Which properties helped you most to identify each mineral?

_____

_____

_____

Going Further Scientists also use an acid test to identify minerals. Limestone contains calcium carbonate, which reacts with acid to release carbon dioxide gas. Sedimentary rocks formed in ocean floors often contain limestone from seashells. Perform an acid test using vinegar, which contains acetic acid, and a seashell.

Safety Wear goggles.

You may also test an egg. What do you think the eggshell is made of?

My Hypothesis Is:

_____

My Experiment Is:

_____

_____

My Results Are:

_____

_____

_____

Mineral	Color	Luster	Streak	Hardness	Other
Galena	Silver gray	Shiny like metal	Gray	Scratched by copper and iron	Splits into cube shapes
Pyrite	Brassy yellow	Shiny like metal	Greenish black	Not scratched by testers	Looks like gold; breaks unevenly
Quartz	Colorless, white, pink, purple	Glassy	White	Not scratched by testers	Breaks unevenly
Mica	Colorless, silvery, brown	May look glassy	White	Scratched by fingernail	Splits into thin sheets
Talc	Pale green, white	Pearly, dull, greasy	White	Scratched by fingernail	Flakes or crumbles easily
Feldspar (Orthoclase)	White, gray, yellow, red, brown	Glassy, pearly	White	Not scratched by testers	Splits easily in two directions
Hornblende	Green, black	Glassy	Brown, gray	Not scratched by testers	Splits easily in two directions

Observing the Layering of Sediments

Hypothesize What will happen if you put some rock particles and sand in water? Which will settle first? Last? Do you think the size of the particles matters?

Write a **Hypothesis:**

_____

Materials

- gravel
- spoon
- fine-grained sand
- clear quart jar with a lid, half-filled with water
- goggles

Procedures

Safety Wear goggles.

1. **Make a Model** Put the gravel and sand in the jar of water. Cover it with the lid. Shake the jar. Set it aside.

2. **Predict** What do you think will happen? Write a prediction.

_____

Conclude and Apply

1. **Compare** How did your prediction compare with the results?

_____

2. **Observe** How many layers formed? Which layer settled first? Last?

_____

3. **Infer** How does this illustrate the formation of sedimentary rocks?

_____

Going Further What happens when soil of different compositions mix? Write and conduct an experiment.

My Hypothesis Is: _____

My Experiment Is: _____

My Results Are: _____

Investigate What You Can Learn from Fossils

Hypothesize How can you interpret clues left from millions of years ago? What types of things can you look for in fossils to learn the story they tell?

Write a **Hypothesis:**

_____

_____

Study the drawing of fossilized footprints on page 3 of this Explore Activity. How many animals made them? What do you think happened first? Last?

Materials

• footprint puzzle

Procedures

1. **Observe** Carefully study the footprints. Look for clues in the sizes and types of prints. Think about which were made first, next, and last.

2. **Communicate** Discuss the evidence with your partner. How can you work together to interpret it?

   _____

3. **Draw Conclusions** Record the "story" you think the prints tell.

   _____

   _____

   _____

Conclude and Apply

1. **Infer** How many animals made the tracks? Are all the animals the same kind? How can you tell?

   _____

   _____

2. **Infer** Were all the animals moving in the same direction? How do you know? Which came first? Next? Last?

_____

_____

_____

_____

3. **Compare and Contrast** How does your story compare with those of your classmates? On what points do you agree? Disagree? Be prepared to defend your interpretation with evidence.

_____

_____

Going Further: Problem Solving

4. **Interpret Data** Create your own footprint puzzle on a separate page. Challenge a classmate to figure out the story that the footprints tell.

? Inquiry

Think of your own questions related to interpreting footprints. Can you identify the footprints of common animals?

My Question Is:

_____

How I Can Find Out:

_____

My Results Are:

_____

_____

Making Molds and Casts

Hypothesize What is the difference between a cast and a mold?

Write a **Hypothesis:**

_____

Materials

- seashells
- petroleum jelly
- modeling clay
- container of plaster of Paris

Procedures

1. **Make a Model** Coat a shell with petroleum jelly. Then firmly but gently press the shell into the clay.

2. Carefully remove the shell from the clay. Fill the clay with plaster of Paris.

3. When the plaster has dried, remove it from the clay.

Conclude and Apply

1. **Identify** Which is the mold? Which is the cast?

_____

2. **Compare** How are they similar and different?

_____

3. **Observe** What shell characteristics can you see in the mold? In the cast? Record your observations.

_____

Going Further What features do you think scientists observe in animal casts and molds? Write and conduct an experiment.

My Hypothesis Is: _____

My Experiment Is: _____

My Results Are: _____

Using Numbers

Comparing Sizes

Footprint size gives a good idea of overall size and height. Scientists have determined that the length of a footprint is generally equal to one-quarter the length of the hind-leg bone of the animal that made it. The length of the bone gives a good idea of the animal's overall size. In this activity you will use numbers to determine the approximate lengths of dinosaur leg bones.

Materials

• calculator (optional)

Procedures

1. **Collect Data** The table gives the footprint length of six adult dinosaurs.

A Name of Dinosaur	B Length of Footprint	C Probable Length of Hind-Leg Bone	D Probable Rank in Overall Size
Triceratops	15 inches ($1\frac{1}{4}$ feet)		
Tyrannosaurus	30 inches ($2\frac{1}{2}$ feet)		
Stegosaurus	18 inches ($1\frac{1}{2}$ feet)		
Velociraptor	6 inches ($\frac{1}{2}$ foot)		
Compsognathus	3 inches ($\frac{1}{4}$ foot)		
Ultrasaurus	78 inches ($6\frac{1}{2}$ feet)		

2. **Use Numbers** Determine how to calculate the lengths of the hind-leg bones. Complete column C.

3. **Compare** Rank the dinosaurs in order of probable overall size. Write 1 for the largest and 6 for the smallest in column D.

Conclude and Apply

1. Interpret Data Which dinosaur probably had the largest hind-leg bone? The smallest?

_____

_____

2. Compare Which two dinosaurs were probably close in size? The most different in size?

_____

_____

Design Your Own Experiment

How Do Glaciers Scratch and Move Rocks?

Hypothesize The main component of a glacier is ice. How can a block of ice help shape Earth's surface?

Write a **Hypothesis:**

_____

_____

_____

Materials

- paper towel
- ice cube made with sand
- wood scrap
- clean ice cube
- aluminum foil

Procedures

1. **Predict** Which ice cube do you think is more like a real glacier? Record your prediction and reasons.

   _____

   _____

2. **Use Variables** Think about how you could use the materials to test your ideas. Which ice cube will scratch a surface? Record your observations for each ice cube.

   _____

   _____

   _____

3. **Observe** Which ice cube will leave "rocks" behind? Place the ice cubes on a folded paper towel. Allow them to melt. Observe and record what is left behind.

   _____

   _____

Conclude and Apply

1. Communicate How did each model feel as you rubbed it over
a surface?

_____

_____

2. Observe Which model scratched the foil? The wood? What happened
when you pushed down harder?

_____

_____

3. Infer What made the scratches?

_____

4. Observe What happens to the sand when the ice cube melts?

_____

Going Further: Problem Solving

5. Compare How does this model help you explain how a glacier
scratches and moves rocks?

_____

Inquiry

Think of your own questions related to glaciers. Are materials other than
rocks trapped in glaciers? What happens to them?

My Question Is:

_____

How I Can Test It:

_____

My Results Are:

_____

_____

Defining Terms Based on Observations

Flow of a Glacier

You know what *flow* means. You can see water flow in a stream or down a drain. What do we mean when we say that a glacier flows? In this activity you will make and observe a model to see how glacial ice flows. Then you will be able to describe glacial ice flow based on your experiences and observations.

Materials

- goggles
- prepared cornstarch mixture
- mixture of sand, gravel, and soil
- waxed paper
- metal spoon
- ruler

Procedures

 Safety Wear goggles.

1. **Make a Model** Place a spoonful of the cornstarch mixture on a piece of waxed paper. This represents a glacier. Record what happens.

   _____

   _____

2. **Observe** Place another spoonful on top of the first. This represents new snow. Record what happens.

   _____

   _____

3. Sprinkle some of the sand mixture in a 3-cm band around the edges and on top. Mark the edges of the sand on the waxed paper.

4. **Observe** One at a time, add four more spoonfuls of the cornstarch mixture. After adding each, mark how far the glacier moves and the sand's position.

5. **Observe** Flip the glacier over onto another piece of waxed paper. Measure and draw the bottom.

Conclude and Apply

1. **Explain** Did the sand mixture sprinkled on top of your model in step 3 eventually reach the bottom?

_____

_____

2. **Interpret Data** What do you think happens when a real glacier moves over rocks and boulders?

_____

_____

_____

3. Define *glacial ice flow.*

_____

_____

_____

Investigate What Soil Is Made Of

Hypothesize What kinds of materials do you think make up different soils? How can you separate soil into its different parts?

Write a **Hypothesis:**

_____

_____

Test different soils to find out what they might be made of.

Materials

- 3 types of soil
- eye dropper
- newspaper
- 3 sharp pencils

- hand lens
- water
- paper towel

Procedures

1. Spread the newspaper on a desk or table. Place one soil sample on each paper towel. Put the paper towels on the newspaper.

2. **Observe** Use a pencil to push around the soil a little bit. Observe each sample with the hand lens. Record as many observations as you can of each soil sample.

_____

_____

_____

3. **Classify** Use the pencil tip to classify the particles of each sample into two piles—pieces of rock and pieces of plant or animal material.

4. **Observe** Put four drops of water on each sample. After a few minutes, check which sample leaves the biggest wet spot on the newspaper.

Conclude and Apply

1. Infer What kinds of materials make up each soil sample?

_____

2. Compare How do the particles you sorted in each soil sample compare by size? By color?

_____

3. Observe Describe the properties you observed of each sample.

_____

_____

4. Compare Which sample absorbed the most water? How can you tell?

_____

Going Further: Apply

5. Infer What do you think soil it made of? How do you think it is made?

_____

_____

❓ Inquiry

Think of your own questions related to soil composition. How can you change how much water a soil can absorb?

My Question Is:

_____

_____

How I Can Test It:

_____

_____

My Results Are:

_____

_____

Rate of Water Flow

Hypothesize What variables might affect the rate of water flow through soil?

Write a **Hypothesis:**

_____

Materials

- clay-rich soil
- 2 measuring cups
- sandy soil
- water
- 2 prepared containers
- stopwatch or clock with second hand

Procedures

1. Put one soil sample in each container. Hold the container of sandy soil over a measuring cup. Slowly pour 1 c of water over the soil, and start timing.

2. **Measure** When water drops begin to "hang," record the total time. Determine the amount of water left in the soil. Record your findings.

_____

3. **Repeat** Repeat with the other soil.

Conclude and Apply

1. **Compare** Through which soil did the water pass more quickly? _____

2. **Compare** Through which soil did more water pass? _____

3. **Interpret Data** Can you relate your findings to soil texture?

_____

Going Further How would the addition of humus affect the water flow and absorption rates of the two sample soils? Write and conduct an experiment.

My Hypothesis Is:

_____

My Experiment Is:

_____

My Results Are:

_____

Design Your Own Experiment

What's Inside?

Hypothesize How can you learn about something that you can't see directly?

Write a **Hypothesis:**

_____

_____

Materials

• 3 sealed opaque containers

Procedures

1. What kinds of observations can you make about the objects in the containers? Make a plan with your group. Outline different things you can test. Record your plan.

   _____

   _____

2. **Observe** Make your observations. Be sure not to damage the containers. Each group member should have a turn with each container. Record all the observations.

   _____

   _____

3. **Interpret Data** Look at all your data. Come to a conclusion about what you think might be in each container.

   _____

   _____

Conclude and Apply

1. Infer What do you think is in each container? On a separate page, draw a diagram or model that supports your observations.

_____

_____

2. Communicate Present your observations for each test. Explain how they support your conclusions.

_____

_____

Going Further: Apply

3. Infer In what ways might these types of observation skills help you in everyday life?

_____

_____

Inquiry

Think of your own questions you might like to ask. What decisions might you make today based on something that you can't see or feel directly?

My Question Is:

_____

How Can I Test It:

_____

_____

My Results Are:

_____

_____

Earthquake Vibrations

Hypothesize How do you think the energy of earthquakes travels through Earth?

Write a **Hypothesis:**

_____

_____

_____

Materials

- marble
- pan of water
- newspaper
- flashlight

Procedures

1. Spread out some newspaper to absorb splashed water. Place the pan of water on the newspaper.

2. **Observe** Take turns dropping the marble into the water from a height of about 15 cm (6 in.). Shine the flashlight on the water to help you see what happens more clearly. Record your observations of the wave patterns.

_____

_____

_____

Conclude and Apply

1. **Communicate** What type of wave pattern did the marble create?

_____

_____

2. **Infer** How do you think this pattern might relate to the way earthquake vibrations travel?

_____

_____

Going Further When you raise the marble over the water, you are working against gravity and using energy. This energy is stored in the marble. When the marble is released and drops into the water, this energy is used to move the water. Raising the marble higher, or lifting a heavier marble, requires more energy, so the marble releases more energy as it falls into the water. How would you expect the wave size to change as a marble is dropped from different heights? How would the wave size change if marbles with different weights were dropped from the same height? Relate this information to earthquakes. Write and conduct an experiment.

My Hypothesis Is:

_____

_____

My Experiment Is:

_____

_____

_____

_____

My Results Are:

_____

_____

_____

_____

_____

Investigate the Characteristics of Animals

Hypothesize Animals come in many sizes and shapes, yet they all have certain characteristics. For example, what are the main characteristics of a fish and snail?

Write a **Hypothesis:**

_____

Observe the characteristics of a snail and a fish to compare how they are similar and different.

Materials

- clear container with aquarium water
- goldfish or guppy
- water snail
- fish food
- ruler

Procedures ▨▨ Safety Be careful with live animals.

1. Obtain a beaker with a fish and a snail in it.

2. **Observe** Record the shape and approximate size of both animals. Describe how each animal moves and any other observations that you make.

_____

_____

3. **Observe** Add a few flakes of fish food to the beaker. What do the animals do? Record your observations.

_____

_____

4. **Draw Conclusions** What does the fish eat? The snail?

_____

Conclude and Apply

1. **Identify** What body parts does each animal have? How do they use these parts? _____

_____

_____

2. Compare Compare how the fish and the snail move. Is movement an advantage for the animals? Explain.

_____

_____

3. Infer Do you think the fish and the snail are made of one cell or many cells? Why?

_____

4. Identify What characteristics do the fish and the snail have? Make a list. Compare your list with other groups' lists. Make a class list.

_____

Going Further: Apply

5. Compare How are you similar to the fish and the snail? How are you different?

_____

_____

? Inquiry

Think of your own questions that you might like to test. What are other ways that people move around?

My Question Is:

_____

How I Can Test It:

_____

My Results Are:

_____

_____

Observing

Animal Symmetry

A scientist's most important job is to *observe,* or look closely at, things. When you observe carefully, you often see things that you didn't know were there. You can practice your observation skills by looking for symmetry in different animals.

Procedures

1. Identify Determine whether each animal has no symmetry, spherical symmetry, radial symmetry, or bilateral symmetry.

2. Classify Record your observations in a chart you create in the
space below.

Conclude and Apply

1. Identify Which animal or animals have radial symmetry?
Bilateral symmetry?

_____

_____

2. Infer Which animal or animals have spherical symmetry?
No symmetry?

_____

3. Explain Does an animal with radial symmetry have a front end and a
back end? Explain.

_____

_____

Investigate the Characteristics of Invertebrates

Hypothesize Many of Walcott's fossils were invertebrates. What characteristics do you think invertebrates have?

Write a **Hypothesis:**

_____

Observe some invertebrates to find out what common characteristics they have.

Materials

- living planarian
- petri dish
- toothpick
- living earthworm
- water
- hand lens
- damp paper towel

Procedures

Safety Be careful with live animals.

1. **Observe** Place the worm on the damp paper towel. Get a petri dish with a planarian (plə nâr′ ē ən) in it from your teacher. Observe each organism with a hand lens. Record your observations.

_____

2. **Observe** Gently touch the worm with your finger and the planarian with the toothpick. What do they do? Record your observations.

_____

3. **Observe** What characteristics of the praying mantis and magnified hydra do you observe? Record your observations.

_____

_____

_____

_____

_____

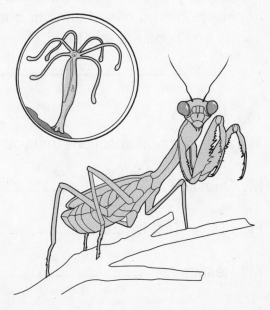

Conclude and Apply

1. **Draw Conclusions** What characteristics do you think invertebrates have? Make a list.

_____

2. **Compare and Contrast** Compare your list with those of other classmates. Based on your observations, make a class list of invertebrate characteristics.

3. **Compare and Contrast** How are Walcott's ancient invertebrates like invertebrates that live today? Do they have similar characteristics? How are they different?

_____

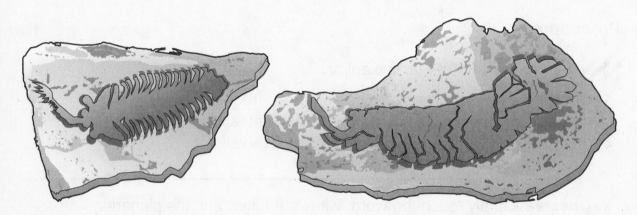

Going Further: Apply

4. **Identify** Think of other organisms that you would classify as invertebrates based on your observations. Make a list. Check your list as you continue this topic.

_____

? Inquiry

Think of your own questions that you might like to test. What size are invertebrates?

My Question Is: _____

How I Can Test It: _____

My Results Are: _____

Classifying Invertebrates

Hypothesize What characteristics would you use to classify these invertebrates?

Write a **Hypothesis:**

_____

_____

Procedures

1. **Identify** Use the clues in each picture to identify which type of invertebrate is shown.

   _____

   _____

   _____

   _____

   _____

   _____

   _____

   _____

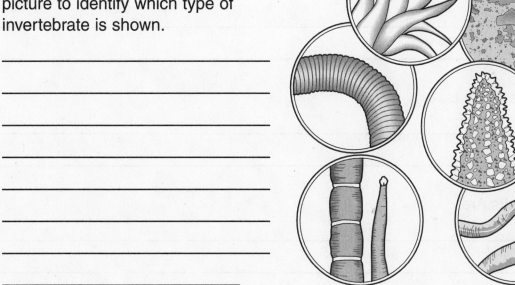

2. **Communicate** Make a table to show how you classified each picture. List key characteristics for each phylum.

Conclude and Apply

Explain How do you know the phylum that each animal belongs to?

_____

_____

Going Further Create a new invertebrate by combining some characteristics of each of the animals in the pictures. Draw the resulting creature. Use another piece of paper to draw the animal. Write and conduct an experiment.

My Hypothesis Is:

_____

_____

My Experiment Is:

_____

_____

My Results Are:

_____

_____

_____

Investigate What Vertebrates Are Like

Hypothesize What characteristics are used to classify vertebrates?

Write a **Hypothesis:**

_____

_____

_____

Observe some vertebrates. What characteristics set each of these animals apart from the others?

Materials

- goldfish
- parakeet
- camera (optional)
- frog
- hand lens
- tape recorder (optional)
- chameleon, turtle, or lizard
- hamster, gerbil, or guinea pig

Procedures ▨▨ Safety Be careful with live animals.

Observe As you observe each animal, look for answers to these questions. Record your observations. If you like, you can record the sounds or take photographs to study the animals better.

   a. Where does it live—in water, on land, or both? _____

   b. What color is it? _____

   c. What kind of outer covering does it have? _____

   d. What body parts does it have?

   _____

   e. Do you see eyes, ears, nostrils, or other sense organs?

   _____

   f. How does it move?

   _____

Conclude and Apply

1. **Communicate** What major characteristics did you observe in
   each animal?

   _____

2. **Compare** What are the main differences between a fish and a frog?

   _____

   _____

3. **Compare** What are the major differences between a bird and a hamster?

   _____

   _____

Going Further: Problem Solving

4. **Identify** Which animal are you most like in this activity? Why do you
   think so?

   _____

   _____

❓ Inquiry

Think of your own questions that you might like to test. Which animal are
you least like in this activity?

My Question Is:

_____

How I Can Test It:

_____

My Results Are:

_____

_____

_____

Classifying Vertebrates

Hypothesize What characteristics would you use to classify these vertebrates?

Write a **Hypothesis:**

_____

_____

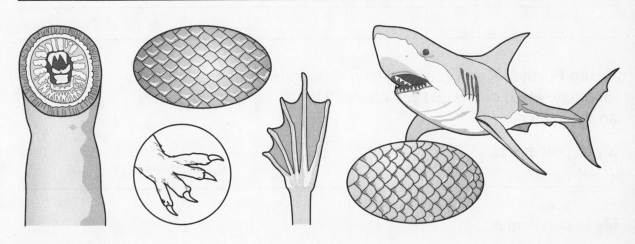

Procedures

1. **Classify** Use the clues in each picture to help you classify each animal.

_____

_____

_____

_____

2. **Communicate** Make a table to show how you classified each picture.

Conclude and Apply

Explain How do you know which class each animal belongs to?

_____

_____

_____

_____

_____

Going Further If you could select a vertebrate characteristic to try for a day, which one would you choose? Why? Write and conduct an experiment.

My Hypothesis Is:

_____

My Experiment Is:

_____

My Results Are:

_____

_____

Investigate How Blood Travels

Hypothesize Which do you think is more complex—a frog's heart or a fish's heart?

Write a **Hypothesis:**

_____

_____

Compare models of fish and amphibian hearts.

Materials

- 5 straws
- two 7-oz cups, each with a hole in the bottom
- three 3-1/2 oz cups, each with a hole in the bottom
- 2 paper circles
- 5 labels
- marking pen
- tape

Procedures

1. Label each small cup "atrium." Label each large cup "ventricle."

2. **Make a Model: Fish Heart** Tape the paper circle with one flap over the top of one ventricle. Center the top of an atrium over the flap in the circle. Tape it to the paper.

3. Label one straw "From gills and body." Place it in the hole in the bottom of the atrium. Label another straw "To gills and body." Place it in the hole in the bottom of the ventricle. Draw the model on a separate piece of paper.

4. **Make a Model: Amphibian Heart** Tape the paper circle with two flaps over the top of a ventricle. Center the top of an atrium over each flap. Tape the cups to the paper.

5. Label one straw "From body." Place it in the hole in the bottom of the right cup. Label another straw "From lungs." Place it in the hole in the bottom of the left cup. Label the third straw "To lungs and body." Place it in the hole in the paper between the two small cups. Draw the model on a separate piece of paper.

Conclude and Apply

Compare and Contrast How are the fish heart and the amphibian heart alike? Different?

_____

_____

_____

_____

Inquiry

Think of your own questions that you might like to test. Which animals have the most complex hearts?

My Question Is:

_____

How I Can Test It:

_____

_____

My Results Are:

_____

_____

Fooling Your Senses

Hypothesize Can your eyes be fooled?

Write a **Hypothesis:**

_____

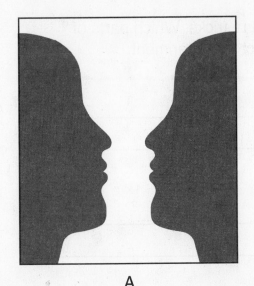

A

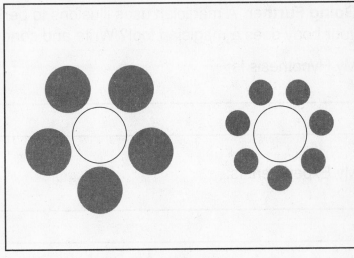

B

Procedures

1. Observe Look at drawing A. What do you see?

_____

_____

2. Observe Observe the center circles in drawing B. Compare their sizes by just observing.

_____

_____

3. Measure Measure each center circle in drawing B. Which circle is bigger?

_____

_____

_____

Conclude and Apply

Draw Conclusions Can your eyes fool you? Explain.

_____

_____

Going Further A magician uses illusions to perform tricks. Which parts of your body does a magician fool? Write and conduct an experiment.

My Hypothesis Is:

_____

_____

My Experiment Is:

_____

_____

My Results Are:

_____

Design Your Own Experiment

How Do Mealworms Change as They Grow?

Hypothesize Do you know of young animals that look very different from their parents? How do you think they change as they grow older?

Write a **Hypothesis:**

_____

_____

Materials

- jars containing food and mealworms in different stages of development
- 3 hand lenses
- 3 rulers

Procedures

1. **Observe** As a group choose a Mealworm Observation Station that your teacher has set up. Each station has three jars labeled A–C.

2. **Observe** Break into smaller groups. Each group should observe the animals in one jar. Record your observations. Share your observations with the other members of your larger group.

   _____

   _____

3. **Ask Questions** Record any questions you have about mealworms and how they change and grow. How could you find the answers?

   _____

   _____

4. **Experiment** Design simple experiments to find out as much as you can about the mealworms. Do they prefer light or dark places? Damp or dry places? Make a group table to display your findings.

5. **Observe** Make observations of the animals every few days. Record your observations. Draw the different stages of development that you observe. Use a separate piece of paper.

Conclude and Apply

1. **Communicate** Describe all the stages of mealworm development.

_____

_____

2. **Draw Conclusions** Use your drawings to arrange the stages in the order in which you think mealworm development occurs.

_____

Going Further: Apply

3. **Compare** How does the way a mealworm grows and changes differ from other animals like cats and dogs?

_____

_____

? Inquiry

Think of your own questions that you might like to test. Do some insects go through changes as they grow?

My Question Is:

_____

_____

How I Can Test It:

_____

_____

My Results Are:

_____

_____

Heredity Cards

Hypothesize How many possible offspring can come from six different traits?

Write a **Hypothesis:**

_____

_____

Materials

- pink construction paper
- scissors
- blue construction paper
- marker

Procedures

1. Cut three cards from each paper. Pink cards represent the female, blue cards the male.

2. Write a trait for "Hair," "Eye color," and "Height" on one set of cards. Make sure the traits on the other set are different.

3. **Collect Data** Match cards to make "offspring." Each offspring needs one card for each trait.

4. **Repeat** Continue matching cards to create offspring. Give each a number. Record the traits in a table. Use another piece of paper for the table.

Conclude and Apply

1. **Observe** How many different offspring did you get? _____

2. **Predict** How many different offspring would you get with eight trait cards?

_____

_____

Going Further Think about a family you know in which there are several children. Is there one trait that all the children have? Is there a trait that only one of the children has? Write and conduct an experiment.

My Hypothesis Is:

_____

_____

My Experiment Is:

_____

_____

My Results Are:

_____

_____

Investigate How Body Color Can Help
an Animal Survive

Hypothesize What role does body color play in the types of places an animal can stay without being noticed?

Write a **Hypothesis:**

_____

_____

Test your ideas by pretending to be a bird searching for worms.
Which color worms are easiest to see?

Materials

• colored toothpicks
• label or piece of masking tape

• plastic bag or shoe box
• marking pen

Procedures

1. Label your bag or box with your name. This is your "nest."
   Use it to hold all the toothpick "worms" that you collect.

2. **Observe** Follow the rules given by
   your teacher to capture the worms.
   Record the rules. Also record any
   observations that you make while
   collecting the worms.

   _____

   _____

   _____

   _____

   _____

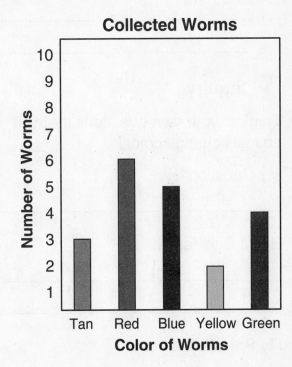

Collected Worms

3. **Communicate** When you are done,
   record your results in a bar graph like
   the one shown.

Conclude and Apply

1. Explain Which color worms were easiest to see? Why?

_____

_____

2. Explain Which color worms were hardest to see? Why?

_____

_____

3. Draw Conclusions If you were to become a toothpick worm, what color would you want to be? Why?

_____

_____

Going Further: Problem Solving

4. Predict Colors help certain animals blend in with their surroundings. Why do you think some animals have bright colors? How could you find out?

_____

_____

❓ Inquiry

Think of your own questions that you might like to test. Why do other animals change color?

My Question Is:

_____

How I Can Test It:

_____

_____

My Results Are:

_____

_____

Forming a Hypothesis

How Do Adaptations Help an Animal Survive?

Every science experiment begins with a hypothesis. A hypothesis is a statement you can test. "Dogs like big bones best" is a hypothesis. You could test this hypothesis by giving dogs different-sized bones.

In this activity you will design two different kinds of animals—a super predator and an animal that is skilled at avoiding predators. Then form a hypothesis about how the adaptations would help each animal in different situations.

Materials

- modeling clay
- construction paper
- drawing materials

Procedures

1. **Plan** What traits should your predator have? Record them. Describe how these traits would help the animal.

   _____

   _____

   _____

2. **Repeat** Do the same for your avoider animal.

   _____

   _____

   _____

3. **Communicate** Make a table like the one shown for each animal. Fill in each category that applies. Add any extra categories that you need.

4. **Make a Model** Make models or colored drawings of your animals. Label all the features of your animals. Tell how they function. Use a separate piece of paper for your drawings.

Animal Name _____

Predator ☐   Avoider ☐

Food _____

Enemies _____

Environment _____

Trait	How it Helps
Length	
Weight	
Shape	
Coloring	
Pattern	
Skin	
Arms	
Legs	
Tails	
Fins	
Eyesight	
Hearing	
Smell	
Strength	
Quickness	
Intelligence	

5. Hypothesize How would these features help the animal survive?

_____

Conclude and Apply

1. Communicate What are the animals' most important features?
How would they use these features?

_____

_____

_____

2. Explain Review your hypothesis. How could you test it?

_____

_____

_____

3. Predict Predict what would happen if you could test your hypothesis.

_____

_____

Investigate What Happens to Rubbed Balloons

Hypothesize What do you think will happen when two rubbed balloons are brought next to each other? Will they pull together or push apart?

Write a **Hypothesis:**

_____

Test what happens when two balloons are brought next to each other.

Materials

- two 9-in.-round balloons, inflated
- tape
- 2 pieces of string, 50 cm each
- wool cloth scrap or old wool sock

Procedures

1. **Observe** What happens to the balloons when you hang them as shown in the picture? Write about it.

_____

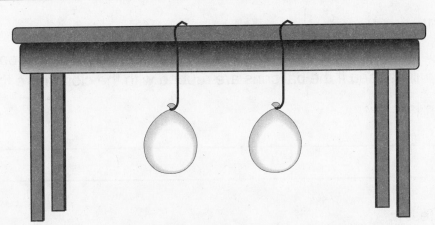

2. **Predict** What will happen if you rub one balloon with a piece of wool? Both balloons? Test your predictions.

_____

3. **Predict** What will happen if you hold the wool cloth between the balloons? Test your prediction.

_____

4. **Predict** What will happen if you put your hand between the two balloons? Test your prediction.

_____

Conclude and Apply

1. **Communicate** What happened when you rubbed one balloon with the wool cloth? Both balloons?

_____

2. **Communicate** What happened when you put the wool cloth between

the balloons? _____

3. **Communicate** What happened when you placed your hand between the

balloons? _____

Going Further: Apply

4. **Experiment** Untie one balloon. Rub it with the wool. Try to stick the balloon to the wall. What happens? Why do you think this happened?

_____

_____

? Inquiry

Think of your own questions that you might like to test using the balloons and wool cloth. What will happen if the balloons are rubbed with the cloth more than once?

My Question Is:

_____

_____

How I Can Test It:

_____

_____

_____

My Results Are:

_____

_____

_____

Testing How Long Charges Last

Hypothesize Dylan plans to rub balloons and stick them to the wall for his 2-hour party. Will they stay up?

Write a **Hypothesis:**

_____

_____

Materials

- 3-in. balloon, inflated
- clock or watch

Procedures

1. Rub the balloon on your shirt or hair. Stick it to the wall.

2. Time how long it takes the balloon to fall. Record the time.

_____

Conclude and Apply

1. **Observe** How long did the balloon stay on the wall?

_____

2. **Interpret Data** Does the electrical charge last long enough to hold the balloons up for Dylan's entire party? Explain.

_____

_____

3. **Infer** Why do you think the balloons fell?

_____

_____

Going Further If a rubbed balloon and an unrubbed balloon were stuck to the wall together, would the two balloons stay on the wall as long as one balloon? Why? Write and conduct an experiment.

My Hypothesis Is:

_____

_____

My Experiment Is:

_____

_____

_____

My Results Are:

_____

_____

Investigate What Makes a Bulb Light

Hypothesize What parts are needed to make a light bulb light? How should they be arranged?

Write a **Hypothesis:**

_____

_____

_____

_____

Test what makes a bulb light by arranging the materials in different ways.

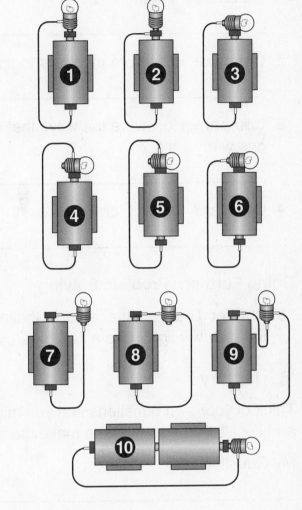

Materials

- flashlight bulb
- 20 cm of wire with stripped ends
- D-cell
- D-cell holder

Procedures

1. **Experiment** Work with your group to try to light the bulb using the materials. Draw each setup. Record your results. Use another piece of paper for drawings.

   _____

2. **Predict** Study the drawings on this page. Predict in which setups the bulb will light and in which it will not light. Record your predictions.

   _____

3. **Experiment** Work with another group of students to test each setup. Can you see a pattern?

   _____

Conclude and Apply

1. **Observe** How many ways could you arrange the materials to make the bulb light in step 1?

   _____

2. **Compare** How were the ways to light the bulb using only one wire similar?

   _____

3. **Compare** How were the ways that did *not* light the bulb using only one wire similar?

   _____

4. **Compare** In which drawings did the bulb light? How are the setups similar?

   _____

Going Further: Problem Solving

5. **Predict** Draw another setup. Challenge a classmate to determine if the bulb will light. Use a separate piece of paper.

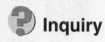 **Inquiry**

Think of your own questions that you might like to test using the bulb, wire, and D-cell. What are ways to make the setup fail?

My Question Is:

_____

How I Can Test It:

_____

_____

My Results Are:

_____

_____

Conductor Test-Off

Hypothesize The base and wires of a light bulb are good conductors. The filament is a poor conductor. What other materials are good conductors or insulators?

Write a **Hypothesis:**

_____

_____

_____

Materials

- flashlight bulb
- bulb socket
- D-cell
- cell holder
- 3 wires with stripped ends, 20 cm each
- assorted test objects

Procedures

1. **Experiment** Make a circuit as shown, using one of the test objects. Record your observations.

_____

_____

2. **Repeat** Test the other objects. Record your observations.

_____

_____

Conclude and Apply

1. **Observe** Which objects were good conductors? Which were not? How could you tell?

_____

_____

_____

2. Infer Examine a length of wire. Which part of the wire is a conductor? Which part is an insulator? Why do you think the wire is made this way?

_____

_____

_____

Going Further If a second wire is connected to the circuit described in the Procedures, would the lightbulb light up? Write and conduct an experiment.

My Hypothesis Is:

_____

_____

My Experiment Is:

_____

_____

_____

My Results Are:

_____

_____

_____

_____

Investigate How to Light Two Bulbs with One Cell

Hypothesize How can you light two bulbs with one cell? Can you have one bulb on and one bulb off?

Write a **Hypothesis:**

_____

_____

Build two different circuits. Observe how electric energy interacts with the parts of a circuit to light bulbs.

Materials

- D-cell
- 2 flashlight bulbs
- 4 pieces of wire with ends stripped, 20 cm each
- cell holder
- 2 bulb holders

Procedures

1. **Experiment** Build a circuit that will light two bulbs. Use one D-cell and the fewest number of wires. Draw it on a separate piece of paper. Label it Circuit 1.

2. **Predict** When both bulbs are lit, predict what will happen if you remove one bulb. Test your prediction. Record your results.

_____

_____

_____

3. **Experiment** Construct another circuit that will light two bulbs. One bulb should remain lit if you remove the other. Draw it on a separate piece of paper. Label it Circuit 2.

4. **Compare** Record in which circuit the bulbs were brighter.

_____

Conclude and Apply

1. Infer Why do you think the bulbs were brighter in one circuit than the other?

_____

2. Compare and Contrast How can removing and replacing a bulb be like opening and closing a switch?

_____

_____

3. Draw Conclusions When you removed a bulb, why did the other bulb go out in one circuit but not in the other?

_____

_____

Going Further: Apply

4. Infer What kind of circuit do you think works best in your home? Why?

_____

_____

? Inquiry

Think of your own questions that you might like to test using the D-cell, cell holder, bulbs, bulb holders, and wire. What would happen if you added a third light bulb to Circuit 1 and Circuit 2?

My Question Is:

_____

How I Can Test It:

_____

_____

My Results Are:

_____

_____

Predicting

Predict If It Will Light

Making predictions is like telling the future. You can't be sure of the future. However, you can sometimes use what you know to make a good prediction.

How do you make good predictions? Look closely at each circuit. How is it similar to circuits you have seen before? How is it different? Use the information in the diagrams to predict what will happen in each circuit.

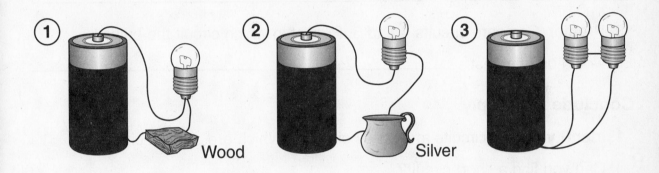

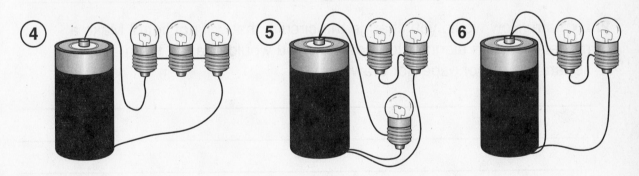

Procedures

1. **Observe** Study each circuit diagram carefully. Think about how current would flow in each circuit.

2. **Predict** In which circuits do you think the bulb or bulbs would light up? Record your predictions in the table on the following page.

Circuit	Prediction
1	
2	
3	
4	
5	
6	

3. Predict Compare circuits 4 and 5. Predict in which circuit the bulbs would be brightest. _____

Conclude and Apply

1. Identify Which circuits are series circuits? Which are parallel circuits? Can you find a short circuit?

_____

_____

2. Explain How would you change the circuits that will not light? Make a model or draw a diagram to show how you would change them. Use a separate piece of paper for drawings.

_____

_____

_____

3. Predict Draw yet another circuit. Challenge a classmate to predict if the bulb or bulbs would light. Ask your classmate to explain his or her thoughts about the prediction. Use a separate piece of paper for drawings.

_____

_____

Investigate How a Bar Magnet Is Like a Compass

Hypothesize How does a bar magnet compare with a compass?
How could you find out?

Write a **Hypothesis:**

_____

_____

_____

Play around with magnets to test how
they compare with a compass.

Materials

• 2 bar magnets

• compass

• tape

• 1 m of string

• ruler

• heavy book

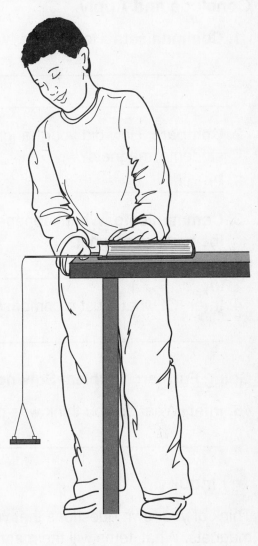

Procedures

1. **Observe** How do the bar magnets
   interact when you place them next to
   each other in different positions?

   _____

   _____

2. **Predict** Which way will the bar
   magnet point if you hang it as shown?
   Record your prediction.

   _____

3. **Observe** Test your prediction. Record the results.

   _____

4. **Compare** Place the compass on a flat surface away from the
   magnets. Compare the directions in which the compass and
   magnet point.

   _____

5. Observe Hold the compass near the hanging magnet. What happens?

_____

Conclude and Apply

1. Communicate How do the two magnets interact with each other?

_____

_____

2. Compare How did your hanging magnet compare with other students' magnets?

_____

3. Communicate What happened when you brought the compass near the hanging magnet?

_____

4. Infer Of what must a compass be made?

_____

Going Further: Problem Solving

5. Infer What do you think was pulling the magnet and compass?

_____

❓ Inquiry

Think of your own questions that you might like to test using the bar magnets. What items will the magnets attract?

My Question Is:

_____

How I Can Test It:

_____

My Results Are:

_____

How Magnets Interact

Hypothesize It seems that there is an invisible force at work between magnets. What do you think causes magnets to interact the way they do?

Write a **Hypothesis:**

_____

_____

Materials

- safety goggles
- piece of white paper
- tape
- 2 bar magnets
- iron filings in a sealed plastic bag

Procedures

 Safety Wear safety goggles.

1. **Observe** Tape a bar magnet flat on your desk. Place the paper over it. Put the bag of iron filings over the paper. Sketch the pattern of the filings.

2. **Observe** Repeat step 1 using two bar magnets with their poles 2 cm apart. Try different north/south combinations. Sketch each setup and the patterns you see. Use a separate piece of paper for sketches.

Conclude and Apply

1. Observe Describe the pattern of the filings when like and unlike poles were next to each other.

_____

_____

_____

2. Compare How was the pattern of a single bar magnet different from the pattern of two magnets?

_____

_____

_____

Going Further Will the magnets make the same patterns if the filings are in water? Write and conduct an experiment.

My Hypothesis Is:

_____

_____

My Experiment Is:

_____

_____

My Results Are:

_____

Stronger Electromagnets

Hypothesize What will make an electromagnet stronger?

Write a **Hypothesis:**

_____

_____

Materials

- nail
- wire with stripped ends
- 2 D-cells and holders
- 10 paper clips

Procedures

1. Wind the wire 20 times around the nail near its head. Attach each end of the wire to the D-cell to complete the circuit.

2. **Observe** Record how many paper clips your electromagnet can hold.

   _____

3. **Experiment** Repeat using two D-cells in series. Record how many paper clips the nail held.

   _____

   _____

4. **Experiment** Wind the wire 20 more times. Repeat steps 2 and 3.

   _____

   _____

Conclude and Apply

Interpret Data How did increasing current affect the strength of the electromagnet? Increasing the number of coils?

_____

_____

Going Further Which change has the greater effect—increasing current or adding coils? Explain. Write and conduct an experiment.

My Hypothesis Is:

_____

_____

My Experiment Is:

_____

_____

My Results Are:

_____

_____

Investigate Another Way to Make Electric Current

Hypothesize You know that electric current can produce a magnetic field. Do you think that a magnetic field can produce electric current?

Write a **Hypothesis:**

_____

_____

Test another way to make electric current using wires and a magnet.

Materials

- "current detector"
- bar magnet
- D-cell
- D-cell holder
- tape
- paper-towel tube wrapped with enameled wire

Procedures

1. Turn your "current detector" until the needle points north. Line up the wire loops with the needle. Tape the detector to your desk.

2. **Observe** Connect one end of the wire to the D-cell in its holder. Briefly touch the other end of the wire to the other end of the cell. Record your observations.

   _____

3. Obtain a cardboard tube wrapped in wire from your teacher. Connect the current detector to the ends of the wires to make a circuit.

4. **Observe** Insert the bar magnet into the tube. Observe what happens to the detector.

5. **Predict** What will happen if you take out the magnet? Try it. Record your observations.

   _____

Conclude and Apply

1. **Observe** What happened to the current detector when current passed through the wire?

   _____

2. Interpret Data What did the loops of wire around the compass form when current passed through them?

_____

3. Infer How does the moving compass needle show that current passed through the wire?

_____

_____

_____

Going Further: Problem Solving

4. Infer What made a current in the wire?

_____

_____

❓ Inquiry

Think of your own questions that you might like to test. What would happen if there was an electricity failure?

My Question Is:

_____

How I Can Test It:

_____

_____

My Results Are:

_____

_____

Build a Wet Cell

Hypothesize How do you think you can make a wet cell?

Write a **Hypothesis:**

_____

_____

Materials

- safety goggles
- plastic cup
- zinc strip
- current detector from the Explore Activity
- $\frac{1}{2}$ c of distilled vinegar
- copper strip
- tape

Procedures

Safety Wear safety goggles.

1. Put on your goggles. Pour the vinegar into the cup.

2. **Observe** Tape one metal strip to each end of the current detector. Place the metal strips in the vinegar. Record your observations of the detector.

_____

Conclude and Apply

1. **Observe** Did your wet cell produce current? How do you know?

_____

_____

2. **Communicate** What function did the vinegar have in your experiment?

_____

_____

Going Further What other common liquid acids could you try in place of the vinegar? **Hint**: Acids have a sharp, sour smell. Write and conduct an experiment.

My Hypothesis Is:

_____

_____

My Experiment Is:

_____

_____

My Results Are:

_____

_____

Using Numbers

Transformers and Numbers

Numbers help you understand how things work in the real world. In this activity you will be looking for a pattern in the volts going into and out of five different transformers.

Materials

• calculator (optional)

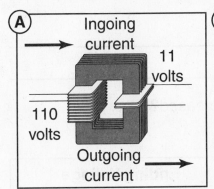

A — Ingoing current — 11 volts — 110 volts — Outgoing current

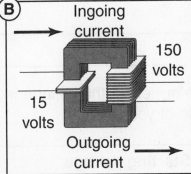

B — Ingoing current — 150 volts — 15 volts — Outgoing current

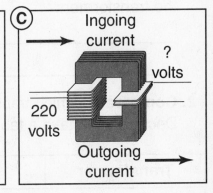

C — Ingoing current — ? volts — 220 volts — Outgoing current

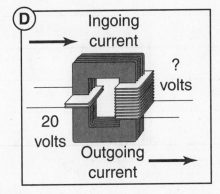

D — Ingoing current — ? volts — 20 volts — Outgoing current

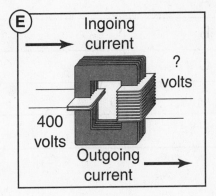

E — Ingoing current — ? volts — 400 volts — Outgoing current

Procedures

1. The left side of transformer A has 10 times as many loops as the right side. Ten times as many volts go into the transformer as go out. The 110 volts going in are reduced 10 times to 11 volts.

2. The right side of transformer B has 10 times as many loops as the left side. Ten times fewer volts go into the transformer as go out. The 15 volts going in are increased 10 times to 150 volts.

3. **Interpret Data** Do you notice a pattern? Write the number of volts for diagrams C–E.

Transformer	Number of Volts
C	
D	
E	

Conclude and Apply

1. Interpret Data What is the pattern that you noticed in the transformers?

_____

_____

2. Compare In which transformers is the voltage increased? Decreased? Make a table of your results.

Transformer	Starting Voltage	Ending Voltage
A		
B		
C		
D		
E		

Design Your Own Experiment

Can Light Energy Change?

Hypothesize Can the light energy of even small flashlight bulbs be changed into heat?

Write a **Hypothesis:**

_____

_____

_____

_____

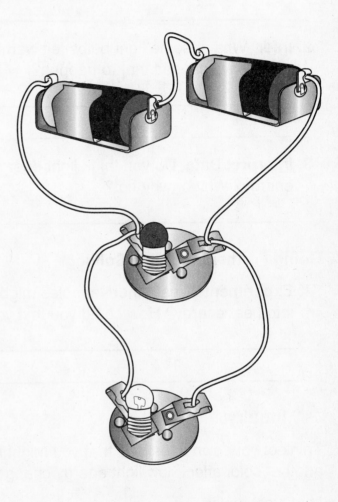

Materials

- flashlight bulb
- flashlight bulb painted black
- 2 bulb holders
- 2 D-cells
- 2 D-cell holders
- small pieces of foil and cloth
- 5 pieces of hookup wire, 20 cm each

Procedures

1. Set up a circuit like this one. You can set up a different circuit if you like.

2. **Use Variables** How would you test to see if painting a bulb affects how warm it gets? Do you think changing the outside of a plain bulb in another way might make it get warmer? Test your ideas. Record your results.

_____

_____

3. **Use Variables** Can you think of any other variable that might affect how warm a bulb gets? Test your ideas. Record your results.

_____

Conclude and Apply

1. Compare Did you feel some heat energy in any of the bulbs? What variables were you testing? What materials were you using?

_____

_____

2. Infer What if some light bulbs felt warmer? How can you explain what might have caused that to happen?

_____

_____

3. Interpret Data Do you think light energy can be transformed into heat energy? Why or why not?

_____

Going Further: Problem Solving

4. Experiment What other variables might affect changing light energy into heat energy? How could you test your idea in an experiment?

_____

_____

❓ Inquiry

Think of your own questions that you might like to test. Would bulbs painted another color affect how light energy changes into heat energy?

My Question Is:

_____

How I Can Test It:

_____

_____

My Results Are:

_____

Identifying Energy Transformations

Hypothesize What types of clues can you use to identify types of energy transformations in your classroom?

Write a **Hypothesis:**

_____

_____

Procedures

1. **Observe** Look around the classroom. Which items use electrical energy? Make a list.

   _____

   _____

   _____

2. **Infer** Which items change electrical energy into another form of energy? What type of energy? Record your observations.

   _____

   _____

   _____

3. **Classify** Classify the items into groups based on how they change electrical energy.

   _____

   _____

   _____

Conclude and Apply

1. **Identify** Into what types of energy did the items change electrical energy?

   _____

   _____

   _____

2. Explain What clues did you use to help you identify how the electrical energy was changed?

_____

_____

Going Further What are some items that change electrical energy into two or more forms of energy? Name the types of energy. Write and conduct an experiment.

My Hypothesis Is:

_____

_____

My Experiment Is:

_____

_____

_____

My Results Are:

_____

_____

_____

Investigate Where Water Can Be Found

Hypothesize Imagine a stegosaur drinking from a pond millions of years ago. What happened to the pond?

Write a **Hypothesis:**

_____

_____

Make a water path to find out about the state of water in different places.

Materials

• 6 different-colored markers   • white drawing paper

Procedures

1. Form six teams; one team at each location. Record your location. What is the state of the water there? Remember, the states of matter are liquid, solid, and gas.

_____

2. Next, each team will go to the next closest location. Record the location and the state of the water. Repeat until every team has visited all six locations.

3. Compare How did the state of water differ from location to location?

_____

_____

4. Interpret Data Use your color markers to draw your team's water path.

Conclude and Apply

1. **Predict** Where might water stay in one place for a short time?
A long time? Why?

_____

_____

_____

2. **Draw Conclusions** Do you think water that was around at the time of
the dinosaurs can still be around today? Why or why not?

_____

_____

_____

Going Further: Apply

3. **Infer** What might have caused the change in the state of water from
place to place?

_____

❓ Inquiry

Think of your own questions that you might like to test. How does water
return to the atmosphere?

My Question Is:

_____

How I Can Test It:

_____

_____

My Results Are:

_____

_____

Communicating

Comparing Amounts of Water

Graphs are another good way to communicate information. Graphs can help you compare information quickly and easily. A pictograph is one kind of graph. It uses a picture symbol to stand for a certain amount of something.

Make a pictograph to compare the amounts of water in different places. Use the information in the table below.

Procedures

1. Suppose that all the water on Earth could be contained in 100 buckets.

2. **Use Numbers** On a separate sheet of paper, make a pictograph to compare the amounts of water in different places. Use the information in the table below. Show how much water is found in different places on Earth. Choose a symbol to stand for 1/100 of all of Earth's water.

Places Where Water Occurs	Amount of Water (part of the total water on Earth)
Oceans and seas	97/100
Glaciers and ice caps	2/100
Soil water and groundwater; lakes, ponds, rivers, and streams; atmosphere; plants and animals	1/100

3. Give your pictograph a title at the top.

4. Be sure to show what the picture symbol stands for.

Conclude and Apply

1. Interpret Data How many symbols did you draw to show the amount of water in glaciers and ice caps?

_____

2. Compare How much more water is found in oceans and seas than in glaciers and ice caps?

_____

3. Communicate How are pictographs similar to charts? How are they different?

_____

_____

_____

Water in an Apple

Hypothesize Write the amount of water you think is in an apple.

Write a **Hypothesis:**

_____

_____

Materials

- apple slices
- tray
- pan balance

Procedures

1. **Measure** Measure the mass of the apple slices, and record the mass.

_____

2. Lay the apple slices on the tray, and place them in a warm place.

3. **Measure** When the slices are completely dried, measure their mass. Record the mass of the dry slices.

_____

_____

Conclude and Apply

1. **Measure** What was the mass of the apple before and after drying?

_____

2. **Use Numbers** How much of the apple's mass was water?

_____

_____

Going Further What other fruits have water? Write and conduct
an experiment.

My Hypothesis Is:

_____

My Experiment Is:

_____

_____

My Results Are:

_____

_____

Investigate What Makes Water Disappear

Hypothesize Where does puddle water go? How long does it take a small puddle to disappear? A big puddle? What causes the water to disappear?

Write a **Hypothesis:**

_____

_____

Experiment to find out how long it takes puddles of water to disappear.

Materials

- measuring cup
- 2 index cards
- water
- 2 lunch trays with sides

Procedures

1. **Measure** Pour a half cup of water into each tray.

2. Place one tray in a sunny area. Place the other in a dark area.

3. Use an index card for each tray. Label one card Sunny and the other card Dark. On each index card, write your name and the date. Then write the time when you placed your trays in each area.

4. **Observe** Check your trays every hour until the water is gone. Note on the index cards how long it took for each "puddle" to disappear. Record your results in the table below.

Time	Observation of Sunny Tray	Observation of Dark Tray

Conclude and Apply

1. Compare Which puddle disappeared first? Which took the longest
to disappear?

_____

_____

_____

2. Draw Conclusions What do you think made one puddle disappear
faster? The other disappear slower?

_____

_____

Going Further: Problem Solving

3. Experiment Repeat the activity, placing your trays in different places.
How were the results similar or different?

_____

_____

❓ Inquiry

Think of your own questions that you might like to test using the water and
lunch trays. What will happen to the water if the tray is covered?

My Question Is:

_____

_____

How I Can Test It:

_____

_____

My Results Are:

_____

Disappearing Water

Hypothesize What happens when a glass of water is left uncovered?

Write a **Hypothesis:**

_____

_____

Materials
• water
• 2 plastic cups
• rubber band
• piece of clear plastic wrap
• marker

Procedures

1. Fill both plastic cups half full with water. Cover one cup with plastic wrap. Use a rubber band to hold down the plastic. Mark the level of the water in each cup.

2. Place both cups in a warm, sunny spot.

3. **Predict** What do you think will happen to the water in each cup?

_____

4. **Observe** Check the water in the cups every hour. Record what you see.

_____

Conclude and Apply

1. Explain Where did the water in each cup go?

_____

_____

2. Infer Why do you think this happened?

_____

_____

_____

_____

Going Further What would happen if you repeated the experiment using ice cubes instead of water? Write and conduct an experiment.

My Hypothesis Is:

_____

_____

My Experiment Is:

_____

_____

My Results Are:

_____

_____

Investigate What Makes the Ocean Move

Hypothesize How could a message in a bottle travel across the ocean?

Write a **Hypothesis:**

_____

_____

Make a model to find out how water temperature affects the way ocean water moves.

Materials

- clear-plastic shoe box
- small plastic sandwich bag
- dropper
- food coloring
- 2 or 3 ice cubes
- room temperature tap water
- twist tie
- small rocks
- 500 mL of very warm tap water
- goggles

Procedures

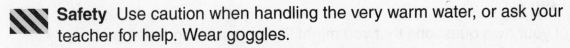 **Safety** Use caution when handling the very warm water, or ask your teacher for help. Wear goggles.

1. Fill the box three-fourths full of room temperature tap water.

2. Put the rocks in the bag. Fill the bag half full of very warm water. Close it with the twist tie.

3. Place the bag in one corner of the box.

4. Float the ice cube in the opposite corner from the bag. If the ice cube melts, put another one in its place.

5. Put food coloring in the dropper. Then place four drops of the coloring in the water next to the ice cube.

6. **Observe** Look at the food coloring for several minutes through the sides of the box. Record what you see.

_____

_____

_____

Conclude and Apply

1. Observe Where did the water sink? Where did it rise?

_____

_____

2. Explain Why do you think you added food coloring to the water?

_____

_____

Going Further: Problem Solving

3. Experiment Repeat the activity without using very warm water. Compare your results. What are some strengths and weaknesses of this model?

_____

_____

Inquiry

Think of your own questions that you might like to test using the shoe box, water, and food coloring. What are other factors that could affect the way ocean water moves?

My Question Is:

_____

_____

How I Can Test It:

_____

_____

My Results Are:

_____

Make Waves!

Hypothesize How does the wind affect waves?

Write a **Hypothesis:**

_____

_____

Materials

- clear-plastic shoe box
- water
- 2 straws
- cork

Procedures

1. Fill the plastic shoe box halfway with water.

2. Place the cork at one end of the box. Take turns quickly puffing through a straw on the water at the other end of the box. Be sure you each use a fresh straw.

3. **Observe** Watch the action of the waves, and record your findings.

_____

4. **Experiment** Puff on the water surface harder and at different distances.

Conclude and Apply

1. Observe Describe how the cork moved in the water.

_____

_____

2. Communicate Use a separate sheet of paper to draw a diagram showing the cork's movements.

Going Further Describe how the cork moves if you and your partner both puff through a straw from opposite ends of the box. Write and conduct an experiment.

My Hypothesis Is:

_____

_____

My Experiment Is:

_____

_____

_____

My Results Are:

_____

_____

Investigate How Fast Water Flows
in Soil and Rocks

Hypothesize How do you think water travels through soil and rocks?

Write a **Hypothesis:**

_____

_____

Test how fast water flows through different materials.

Materials

- cup of perlite or soil
- pencil
- 1 L of water
- cup of marbles

- two 12-oz paper cups
- plastic container
- measuring cup
- stopwatch

Procedures

1. With a pencil tip, make a small hole in the bottom of one paper cup.

2. Place your finger over the hole. Fill the cup with perlite or soil. Hold the cup over a plastic container. Have your partner pour in water to cover the perlite or soil.

3. **Observe** Take away your finger. Time how long it takes the water to drain. Record the results.

_____

_____

_____

4. **Repeat** Repeat using marbles.

_____

_____

Conclude and Apply

1. Identify Which material let water soak through faster?

_____

2. Explain How does the kind of material affect how fast water flows through it?

_____

_____

3. Infer What happens to rainwater falling on soil?

_____

_____

Going Further: Apply

4. Draw Conclusions What can you say about the type of soil that probably is found where wells are dug?

_____

_____

_____

Inquiry

Think of your own questions that you might like to test using the water, paper cups, and other materials. How fast would the water flow through other soil types?

My Question Is:

_____

How I Can Test It:

_____

_____

My Results Are:

_____

Make Runoffs

Hypothesize How do different soils affect runoff?

Write a **Hypothesis:**

_____

_____

_____

_____

SAND

Materials

- two 1-qt milk cartons
- sand
- measuring cup
- plastic tray with sides
- marker
- scissors
- soil
- 1 L of water

Procedures

 Safety Be careful using scissors.

1. Cut the milk cartons as shown. Label one Soil and the other Sand. Place them on the tray.

2. Put an equal amount of sand and soil in the cartons.

3. Fill the measuring cup with water. Slowly pour it over the soil until the soil can hold no more water. Determine the volume of water you poured into the soil. Record it.

_____

_____

4. **Repeat** Repeat Step 3 for the sand.

_____

_____

Conclude and Apply

Compare Which absorbed the most water? Which had the most runoff?

_____

_____

_____

_____

Going Further You inherit a map with an X marking where buried treasure is located. When you arrive at the spot, you discover it is near the ocean. Would you hope that the treasure was buried under dry or wet soil? Why? Write and conduct an experiment.

My Hypothesis Is:

_____

_____

My Experiment Is:

_____

_____

_____

My Results Are:

_____

_____

Using Variables

Surface Area and Evaporation

Variables are things, or factors, in an experiment that can be changed to find answers to questions. In this activity you'll answer this question: Does size or surface area of a puddle affect how fast it will evaporate. For a fair test, all of the factors in the experiment must remain the same. The only variable is surface area.

Materials

- water
- small box of paper clips
- scissors
- measuring cup
- whole kitchen sponge
- pan balance
- spotlight lamp
- half kitchen sponge

Procedures

1. **Make a Model** Use the sponges to make models of puddles with different surface areas.

2. Place one sponge in each pan of the balance. Add paper clips to the pan with the smaller sponge until both sides of the balance are equal in mass.

3. **Infer** Find a way to add equal amounts of water to both sponges.

4. **Observe** Once you have set up your models, turn on the lamp. Check the models every half-hour. Record your observations in the table below.

Time	Observations

Conclude and Apply

1. **Infer** Which model became lighter first? What does this tell you about surface area and evaporation?

_____

_____

_____

2. **Identify** What variables did you change? Keep the same?

_____

_____

_____

3. **Experiment** What could you do to make water evaporate faster? Slower? Test your ideas.

_____

_____

_____

Design Your Own Experiment

How Much Fresh Water Is Used?

Hypothesize People use—and waste—fresh water every day. How can you find out how much water is used at your school each day?

Write a **Hypothesis:**

_____

_____

Materials

- two 9-ounce plastic cups
- stopwatch, clock, or watch with second hand
- measuring cup
- calculator (optional)

Procedures

1. **Plan** Determine ways to measure or estimate the amount of water used daily in school.

   _____

   _____

2. **Collect Data** How can you figure out how much water is being used by each student? By each class?

   _____

   _____

   _____

3. **Communicate** Design a table to record all the data you gathered from your investigation.

Conclude and Apply

1. **Compare** Which activities used the most water each day? Which
   used the least? _____

   _____

2. **Use Numbers** How can you estimate how much water is used in the
   whole school in a day? _____

   _____

3. **Infer** From your observations can you think of ways to save water?

   _____

Going Further: Apply

4. **Communicate** What is another way to record the data you collected?
   Think about a way to present the information clearly.

   _____

   _____

   _____

   _____

Inquiry

Think of your own questions that you might like to test. Where else is water
used in large amounts?

My Question Is:

_____

How I Can Test It:

_____

_____

My Results Are:

_____

Wasted Water

Hypothesize Can you estimate how much water a leaky faucet might waste in a day?

Write a **Hypothesis:**

_____

_____

Materials

• 1,000-mL (1-L) pitcher
• water faucet
• clock or watch with second hand
• calculator (optional)

Procedures

1. Turn on the faucet until it drips slowly.

2. **Collect Data** Place the pitcher under the faucet for five minutes.

3. **Measure** Measure the collected water. Record the amount.

_____

_____

Conclude and Apply

1. **Observe** How much water was wasted in five minutes?

_____

2. **Use Numbers** If the faucet dripped like this every day, how much water would be wasted in an hour? In a day? In a week? In a year?

_____

_____

_____

Going Further If the faucet has dripped like this every day, how much
water would have been wasted since you were born? Write and conduct
an experiment.

My Hypothesis Is:

_____

_____

My Experiment Is:

_____

_____

My Results Are:

_____

Design Your Own Experiment

How Important Is a Supporting Frame?

Hypothesize Do you think a supporting frame is important to a building? Why or why not?

Write a **Hypothesis:**

_____

_____

_____

Materials

- construction paper
- glue or tape
- scissors
- blocks, straws, or craft sticks
- any other building supplies you choose

Procedures

▧▧▧ **Safety** Use the scissors carefully!

1. **Communicate** Work as a class to design a model of a simple building. Copy it on another sheet of paper.

2. **Make a Model** Work with your group to design and build a frame for it. Use any materials you like. Paper can be used for the walls and roof. Record your design on another sheet of paper.

3. **Make a Model** Build another model of the same building, but without a frame.

4. **Communicate** Work as a class to design a way to test the strength of each model.

5. **Collect Data** Test the strength of your models. Record the results.

_____

_____

Conclude and Apply

1. **Compare** Which model was stronger?

_____

2. **Compare and Contrast** Which model was the strongest in the entire class? What was it made of? How was it built?

_____

_____

3. **Draw Conclusions** What conclusions can you draw about the importance of a strong supporting frame?

_____

Going Further: Apply

4. **Experiment** If you could redesign the frame, how would you change it? Why? Build and test your new design. Is it stronger?

_____

_____

❓ Inquiry

Think of your own questions that you might like to test. Can the materials you used in your frame support a larger model?

My Question Is:

_____

How I Can Test It:

_____

_____

My Results Are:

_____

_____

Measuring

Measuring and Comparing Body Parts

"The length from heel to toe is equal to the length from elbow to wrist." Do you think this statement is true? How could you find out? In this activity you will use a ruler to measure the length of different body parts. You will create a bar graph of your results. Then you will use the graph to look for relationships between the lengths of different body parts.

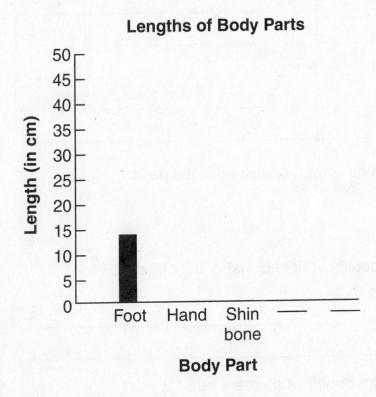

Lengths of Body Parts

Materials

• ruler   • meter tape   • graph paper

Procedures

1. **Collect Data/Measure** Take turns measuring as many different body parts as you can. Ask your partner to help you. Record the data in the table on the next page.

Body Part	Length (cm)

2. Communicate Complete the bar graph on the previous page by plotting the data you collected.

Conclude and Apply

1. Identify Use your graph to identify your shortest and longest body parts.

_____

_____

2. Compare and Contrast Is the original statement true for you? Your partner?

_____

_____

3. Identify Study both of your graphs. Can you find any patterns in the lengths of body parts? For example, are both of your middle fingers longer than your index fingers?

_____

_____

_____

_____

Investigate How Muscles Move Bones

Hypothesize How do you think muscles work to move bones?

Write a **Hypothesis:**

_____

_____

Use a model to test how muscles move bones.

Materials

- 2 equal-length pieces of string
- construction paper
- paper fastener

- tape
- ruler

- cardboard
- scissors

Procedures

Safety Use the scissors carefully!

1. **Collect Data** Measure the lengths of a group member's upper and

   lower arm bones. Record the data. _____

   _____

2. **Measure** Cut the cardboard pieces to the same lengths as the arm bones. Trace a hand on the paper. Cut it out.

3. **Make a Model** Assemble the model as shown.

4. **Experiment** Lay the model on a desk. Hold where indicated. Pull the top string gently in the direction shown. Then pull the bottom string. Record your observations.

   _____

   _____

   _____

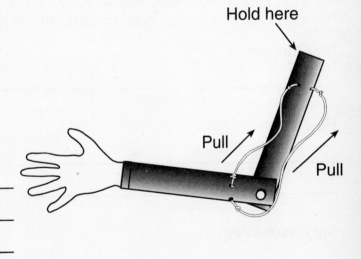

Hold here

Pull

Pull

Conclude and Apply

1. Identify Which parts of your model represent bones? Muscles?

_____

_____

2. Communicate What happened to the "arm" when you pulled the top string? The bottom string?

_____

_____

3. Communicate What happened to the bottom string when you pulled the top string? To the top string when you pulled the bottom string?

_____

Going Further: Apply

4. Experiment Build and test a model of the leg and knee joint. How is it similar to the arm model? Different? What are its strengths and weaknesses? _____

_____

_____

Inquiry

Think of your own questions that you might like to test about how muscles move bones. Are bones in other parts of the body moved in similar ways?

My Question Is:

_____

How I Can Test It:

_____

_____

My Results Are:

_____

_____

Using Muscles

Hypothesize Do you think you used more voluntary or involuntary muscles in the past half-hour? Why do you think so?

Write a **Hypothesis:**

_____

_____

Procedures

Think about all the ways you used muscles in the past half-hour. Record the information in the chart.

MUSCLES USED IN THE LAST HALF-HOUR			
Muscles Used	**Activity**	**Voluntary Muscle**	**Involuntary Muscle**
Arm muscles	raising hand in class	√	
Eyelids	blinking	√	√

Conclude and Apply

1. Interpret Data How many different ways did you use your muscles?

_____

_____

_____

2. Interpret Data Did you use more voluntary or involuntary muscles? Did you use any muscles that are both voluntary and involuntary? What were they?

_____

_____

_____

Going Further Which do you think you use more often: your breathing muscles or your blinking muscles? Design an experiment to find out.

My Hypothesis Is:

_____

_____

My Experiment Is:

_____

_____

My Results Are:

_____

Investigate Why People Might Use Alcohol and Tobacco

Hypothesize How might advertisements convince someone to start using alcohol or tobacco?

Write a **Hypothesis:**

_____

_____

_____

Examine how ads for alcohol and tobacco try to convince people to use the products.

Materials

• magazine and newspaper ads for alcohol and tobacco products
• paper

Procedures

1. **Classify** Sort the ads into two groups—alcohol and tobacco.

2. **Collect Data** On separate sheets of paper, write down any television ads for beer you can remember. Also write down any alcohol and tobacco ads you remember from billboards. Add the notes to the groups.

_____

_____

_____

_____

3. **Observe** What are people in the ads doing? How old are they? What race and gender are they? What other things do you notice? Record your observations.

_____

_____

_____

_____

Conclude and Apply

1. **Draw Conclusions** What ad features might convince people to use the products?

_____

_____

_____

2. **Make Decisions** Choose two ads that best represent your findings.

3. **Communicate** Share your group's observations with your class. Use the two ads to illustrate your findings.

4. **Communicate** Make a class list of ways the ads try to convince people to use the products.

Going Further: Apply

5. **Ask Questions** What questions do you have about how alcohol and tobacco affect the body that are not answered by the ads? Make a list. Look for answers as you continue this topic.

_____

_____

_____

Inquiry

Think of your own questions that you might like to test about opinions concerning alcohol and tobacco. What do people think about the popularity of these products?

My Question Is:

_____

How I Can Test It:

_____

_____

My Results Are:

_____

Interpreting Data

Compare Smoking Now and in the Past

Do you think fewer people smoke now than in the past? To answer this question, you will interpret data. When you interpret data, you use information from a picture, a table, or a graph. Interpret the data in the graph to answer the question.

Procedures

1. **Classify** What type of graph is used to show the data?

   _____

   _____

2. **Collect Data** In the year 1979, about how many men out of every 100 smoked? In 1985? In 1995? Record the data.

   _____

   _____

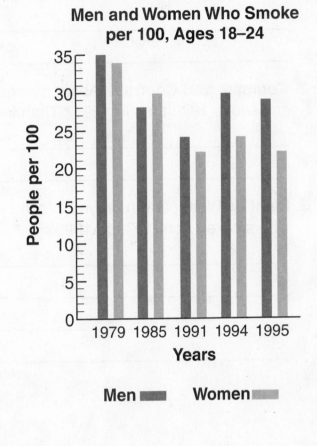

Men and Women Who Smoke per 100, Ages 18–24

People per 100 / Years

Men ▬ Women ▬

3. **Use Numbers** In the year 1979, about how many women out of every 100 smoked? In 1985? In 1995?

_____

Conclude and Apply

1. **Compare and Contrast** Did more or fewer men smoke in 1995 than in 1979? Did more or fewer women smoke in 1995 than in 1979?

_____

_____

2. **Compare and Contrast** About how many more men out of every 100 smoked in 1979 than in 1991? Than in 1995?

_____

_____

3. **Identify** What pattern do you see in the number of men and women who smoked from 1979 to 1995?

_____

_____

_____

_____

Investigate How Medicines Are Similar and Different

Hypothesize How do you think medicines are similar and different?

Write a **Hypothesis:**

_____

_____

_____

Examine medicine labels to determine a difference in how medicines can be obtained.

Materials

• 4 empty medicine bottles with labels

Procedures

1. **Observe** Carefully observe the bottles and labels. How are they similar? Different? Record your observations.

_____

_____

2. **Observe** What types of information can be found on the labels? Make a list.

_____

_____

3. **Compare** How are the labels different? What seems to be the major difference?

_____

_____

4. **Classify** Use this difference to classify the bottles into two groups.

_____

_____

Conclude and Apply

1. Draw Conclusions How are the two groups similar? How are

they different? _____

_____

2. Compare and Contrast Compare your observations with other

groups. On what do you agree? Disagree? _____

_____

3. Communicate Make a class list of information you collected from the labels

in each group. _____

_____

_____

_____

Going Further: Apply

4. Infer Why do you think it is important to carefully read all

medicine labels? _____

_____

? Inquiry

Think of your own questions that you might like to test about prescription
medicines. How well do people read labels?

My Question Is:

_____

How I Can Test It:

_____

_____

My Results Are:

_____

Help Use Drugs Safely

Hypothesize People can easily misuse a drug. Maybe they did not understand the directions. Maybe they did not read the label at all. What could you do to a drug label to help people not misuse the product?

Write a **Hypothesis:**

_____

Materials

• paper   • coloring pens or pencils

Procedures

1. **Predict** Make a list of things you think might improve a drug's label to help avoid misuse. Record your ideas.

_____

2. **Make a Model** Create a drug label showing your ideas.

3. **Collect Data** Present your model to other groups. Do they think your ideas might help? Record the responses.

_____

Conclude and Apply

1. **Draw Conclusions** Make a class list of the label ideas. Which two ideas seem to be the most effective? Why?

2. **Compare** How do these ideas compare with your hypothesis?

_____

Going Further What kinds of information should a medicine label contain? Write and conduct an experiment.

My Hypothesis Is:

_____

My Experiment Is:

_____

My Results Are:

_____